SEMINAR

General

# Spain in the Seventeenth Century

## Graham Darby

LONGMAN
London and New York

Longman Group Limited,
*Longman House, Burnt Mill, Harlow,*
*Essex CM20 2JE, England*
*and Associated Companies throughout the world.*

Published in the United States of America
by Longman Publishing New York.

First published 1994
Second impression 1995.

*Set in 10/11 point Baskerville (Linotron)*
*Produced through Longman Malaysia, PA*

ISBN 0 582 07234 4

**British Library Cataloguing in Publication Data**
Darby, Graham
    Spain in the Seventeenth Century. –
    (Seminar Studies in History)
    I. Title   II. Series
    946.051                                    94-1990
    ISBN 0-582-07234-4                   CIP

**Library of Congress Cataloging-in-Publication Data**
Darby, Graham.
    Spain in the seventeenth century/Graham Darby.
       p.   cm. — (Seminar studies in history.)
    Includes bibliographical references and index.
    ISBN 0-582-07234-4 : £4.75
    1. Spain—History—House of Austria, 1516 –1700.   I. Title.
II. Series.
DP171.D37   1994                                 94-1990
946'.051—dc20                                     CIP

# Contents

*Contents*

# List of maps

# A note on currency

*Maravedí*:  The basic unit of-account.
*Real*:  Silver coin worth 34 *maravedís*.
*Ducado*:  Ducat. A unit of account equal to 375 *maravedís*.
*Escudo*:  A gold coin worth 440 *maravedís* from 1609 but in Castilian
  accounts generally referred to as the *escudo de diez reales* worth
  340 *maravedís*.
*Peso*: American treasure was expressed in pesos: 272 *maravedís*.
*Vellón*: A fractional coin of silver and copper which eventually
  became all copper.

The ducat 'was used only in payments inside Castile, to calculate
*vellón*, which had no currency outside Castile. Payments in silver
were virtually all made outside Castile and were reckoned in
*escudos*, which were theoretically worth fewer *maravedís* than the
ducat but which in practice came to be about the same value, so
that estimates in *asientos* use both ducats and *escudos*' (**21**, p. XII).

The Portuguese *cruzado* was worth about 15–20 per cent less
than the Castilian ducat; the Neapolitan ducat about 30 per cent
less. There were 3 to 4 *livres tournais* (the French money of
account) to the ducat, and about 3 ducats to the pound sterling.
Rates, of course, varied.

See also (**33**, **35** and **67**).

# Acknowledgements

I would like to thank the Head Master, Mr Tommy Cookson, and the Governors of King Edward VI School, Southampton, for granting me a leave of absence to write this book. On my sabbatical I enjoyed the hospitality of the University of Southampton and Trinity College, Oxford. The University Library at Southampton has been particularly helpful to me. I would also like to thank Dr Kevin Sharpe and Dr Alastair Duke, and Professor J. H. Elliott, for their helpful criticisms of several chapters, and Dr Norman Ball for his friendly advice on the book in its entirety. Roger Lockyer deserves a special mention for all his skill in cutting the manuscript down to size; and finally I must thank my wife, Rose, for putting the text on disk, and my daughters, Natalie and Charlotte, for not erasing it.

Cover: Equestrian portrait of the Duke of Lerma by Peter Paul Rubens. Prado, Madrid. Photo: Bridgeman Art Library.

**To the memory of my father, Henry Joseph Darby (1918–1986)**

# Seminar Studies in History

## Introduction to the series

Under the editorship of a distinguished historian, *Seminar Studies in History* covers major themes in British and European history. The authors are acknowledged experts in their field and the volumes are works of scholarship in their own right as well as providing a survey of current historical interpretations. They are constantly updated, to take account of the latest research.

Each title has a brief introduction or background to the subject, a substantial section of analysis, followed by an assessment, a documents section and a bibliography as a guide to further study. The documents enable the reader to see how historical judgements are reached and also to question and challenge them.

The material is carefully selected to give the advanced student sufficient confidence to handle different aspects of the theme as well as being enjoyable and interesting to read. In short, Seminar Studies offer clearly written, authoritative and stimulating introductions to important topics, bridging the gap between the general textbook and the specialised monograph.

*Seminar Studies in History* were the creation of Patrick Richardson, a gifted and original teacher who died tragically in an accident in 1979. The continuing vitality of the series is a tribute to his vision.

*Roger Lockyer*

## The General Editor

Roger Lockyer, Emeritus Reader in History at the University of London, is the author of a number of books on Tudor and Stuart history, including *Buckingham*, a political biography of George Villiers, first Duke of Buckingham, 1592–1628, and *The Early Stuarts; A Political History of England 1603–1642*. He has also written two widely used general surveys – *Tudor and Stuart Britain* and *Habsburg and Bourbon Europe*.

# Note on the system of references

A bold number in round brackets (5) in the text refers the reader to the corresponding entry in the Bibliography section at the end of the book. A bold number in square brackets, preceded by 'doc'. [doc. 6], refers the reader to the corresponding item in the section of Documents, which follows the main text. Items followed by an asterisk * the first time they appear in the paragraph are explained in the Glossary.

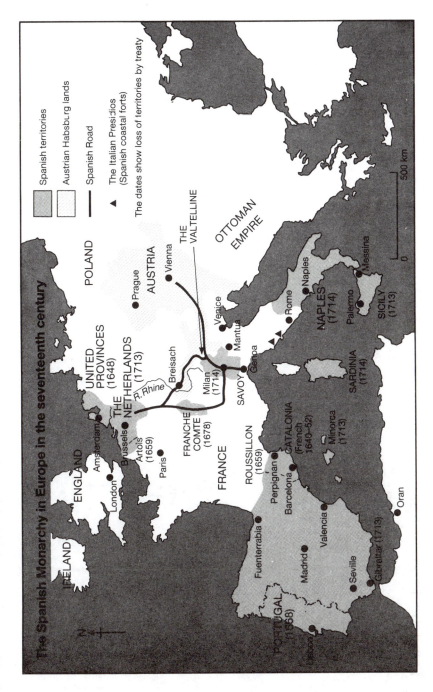

The Spanish Monarchy in Europe in the seventeenth century

Spanish territories

Austrian Habsburg lands

Spanish Road

▲ The Italian Presidios (Spanish coastal forts)

The dates show loss of territories by treaty

0          500 km

IRELAND

ENGLAND

London

UNITED PROVINCES (1648)

THE NETHERLANDS (1713)

Amsterdam

Brussels

Artois (1659)

Paris

FRANCHE COMTE (1678)

FRANCE

POLAND

Prague

AUSTRIA

Vienna

THE VALTELLINE

OTTOMAN EMPIRE

R. Rhine

Breisach

Milan (1714)

SAVOY

Genoa

Mantua

Venice

Rome

Naples

NAPLES (1714)

Palermo

Messina

SICILY (1713)

SARDINIA (1714)

ROUSSILLON (1659)

Perpignan

CATALONIA (French 1640–52)

Barcelona

Minorca (1713)

Fuenterrabia

Madrid

Valencia

Seville

Gibraltar (1713)

Oran

PORTUGAL (1668)

Lisbon

N

ix

# Dynastic Table of Spanish Rulers, 1474 –1700

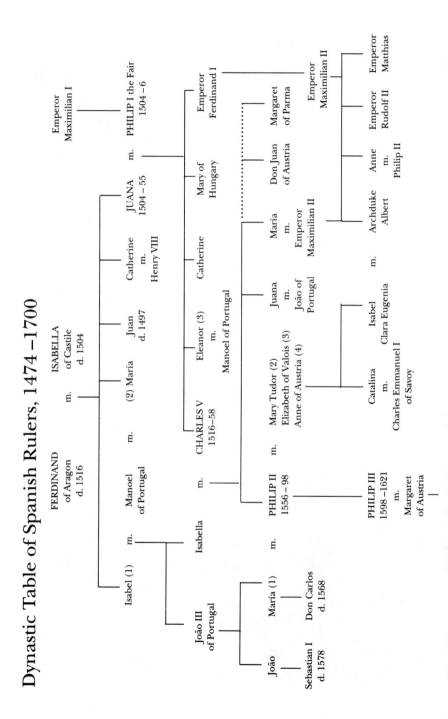

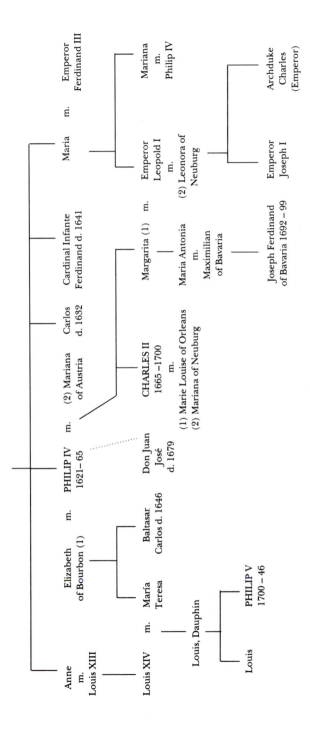

# Part One:   The Background

## 1   The Spanish Habsburg Monarchy

### Origins

At the beginning of the seventeenth century Spain was the foremost power in Europe, if not the world, with territory in northern Europe, Italy, the Mediterranean, the Americas, Africa, India and the Orient. Yet Spain itself was rather unpromising material for greatness; the land was barren, the economy backward and the peninsula was politically fragmented. How, then, had Spain become such a great power? The answer is a complex one, but it was really as a result of dynastic marriage and fortuitous inheritance. The Austrian Habsburg family had inherited the Valois duchy of Burgundy (roughly present-day Holland, Belgium, Luxemburg, and part of Burgundy itself) and the crowns of Aragon (which included the Balearics, Sardinia, Naples and Sicily) and Castile (which included Navarre and the Americas – namely, Mexico and Peru). All this territory came to reside in a single person, Charles Habsburg, the Emperor* Charles V (1519–56), who added the duchy of Milan (see Dynastic Table). This empire had not been planned. It had come about by accident, and from the very beginning it was recognized that it was going to be extremely difficult to hold together. In fact it proved too much for one man, and when Charles abdicated (1555–56) he divided his territories between his brother and his son (the Austrian and Spanish branches, respectively). In this way the Spanish Monarchy (*monarquía española**) emerged as a formidable power in its own right.

Charles's imperial legacy was an enormous burden and represented a distortion in the pattern of interests of the kingdoms of the Iberian peninsula, which had been largely focused on the Mediterranean and America. But although Castile, with its relatively small population and weak economy, did not have the resources to sustain great-power status on its own, when these were allied with the naval expertise and military manpower of Genoa and Naples, Flemish and Milanese weaponry and American silver, it could. In any event we must be careful not to judge the Monarchy from our own perspective of the compact nation state. The Spanish Habsburgs looked upon their network of domains as a family patrimony, and this concept of patrimony was accepted and understood by the elite – the propertied families who cherished their own inheritances in the same spirit (**53**). Moreover, it was not unusual for rulers to have territory separated by large tracts of land or sea, and if their government was remote and undemanding, as it usually was in the Spanish Monarchy, then there was little reason to challenge it. It was attempts at increasing control beyond what was customary which led to unrest and rebellion, as happened with the Dutch in the sixteenth century and the Portuguese and Catalans in the seventeenth.

## Philip II (1556–98)

Unlike his father, Philip saw himself as truly Spanish (or, more correctly, Castilian). He had been born in Castile and spoke only Castilian. 'What had been a polyglot empire administered by a migratory court now became Castilian ruled from a fixed point' (**60**, p. 126). Philip was responsible for considerable achievements: the 'taming of America' and the conquest of the Philippines (from 1565) and Portugal (1580) were outstanding successes; and he built up Spain as a considerable military and naval power. Some historians have gone so far as to describe Philip's reign as the 'zenith' of Spanish power and achievement (for example, Merriman and Ortiz). But this is to underestimate Spain's strength in the seventeenth century (**57, 111**) and to overestimate it in the sixteenth. Only a weak and divided France, after the accidental death of Henry II in 1559, had made Spanish hegemony in Europe possible. Moreover, many of Philip's policies were far from successful and had disastrous consequences. He missed the opportunity for a satisfactory peace with the Turks at the beginning of the reign and lost almost all of North Africa to Islam. He provoked the Dutch into a rebellion which he could not suppress; he attempted to invade England and failed; and although he successfully invaded France he was unable to prevent Henry IV's triumph. He placed an enormous tax burden on the ordinary Castilian (up 430 per cent, 1559–98), yet despite this he seriously overspent, thus creating a cumulative debt of 85 million ducats* (up from 30 million). In this way he paid for defence in the present by mortgaging the future. In many ways Philip II's reign set the agenda for Spanish policy in the seventeenth century; but his legacy of the Dutch rebellion and financial insolvency were to be intolerable burdens.

Philip's ambitious foreign policy had created suspicion among Spain's enemies, and Cardinal Richelieu declared his belief in 1624 that 'one cannot doubt that the Spaniards aspire to universal domination' (quoted in **71**, p. 23). In fact, in the seventeenth century Spanish policy was largely defensive – to maintain the integrity of the dynastic inheritance – but this was easily mis-understood. Keeping open communications between possessions separated by land and sea sometimes involved trespassing on terri-tory in between, and it required an active political interest in neighbouring states which sometimes cut across the interests of other powers. In addition, the King of Spain had interests outside his own patrimony, principally with regard to his Austrian cousins in Vienna, who were also, as Holy Roman Emperors, nominal rulers over Germany. The Spanish Monarchy also had religious interests which were not confined within its boundaries. The Most Catholic King, as the King of Spain was known, was not only concerned to defend Christianity against the Turk and to root out all brands of heterodoxy from his own dominions, but as self-appointed champion of the Counter-Reformation Catholic Church he confronted the rising tide of heresy wherever that might be. The Spanish Habsburgs were also driven by something less easy to gauge – namely, a highly developed concern to preserve their *reputación**. *Reputación* consisted mainly of outward appearances, involving the maintenance of prestige and of face-saving devices to disguise setbacks. It is important to understand this concept since it helps to explain why on many occasions policy would be conceived not in terms of what was realistic but in terms of what was best for the King's *reputación*.

At the beginning of the seventeenth century Spain was still the foremost power in Europe, and although the treaties of 1598 with France, 1604 with England and 1609 with the Dutch may have marked the failure of Philip II's grandiose schemes, they did offer the Monarchy the opportunity for conservation and recuperation. However, as it turned out, the Duke of Lerma's cautious policies (1598–1618) were only to be a short interlude. Under Olivares (1622–43) there was a reversion to the forward policy of Philip II, and the ensuing continual warfare, though it was justified as a defence of essential dynastic, religious and commercial interests, threatened the integrity of the Monarchy. Increased commitments

3

at a time of economic decline made the struggle for survival all the more difficult, leading to a series of setbacks in the 1640s, and, after a brief recovery, a dramatic collapse of power between 1656 and 1668. It was the revival of France that presented Spain with its greatest challenge, and during the course of the century the *monarquía** lost primacy of place to the Bourbons. In 1648 it was compelled to acknowledge the independence of the Dutch, and later that of the Portuguese (1668); in addition, it was forced to cede Roussillon, Cerdagne and Artois (1659), Charleroi, Lille and Tournai (1668), Franche-Comté (1678), and Luxemburg and the County of Flanders (1684) to France (though the last two were returned in 1697). Finally, in 1713/14 the Monarchy was divested of the Spanish Netherlands, Milan, Naples, Sicily, Sardinia, Minorca and Gibraltar. Yet even so, when the Spanish Monarchy was finally broken up in 1713/14 it was for dynastic reasons, the death of the last Habsburg, rather than because of military defeat or economic weakness. It would appear, then, that the reason for the demise of the Spanish Monarchy was very similar to the reason for its rise.

# 2  Government and Resources

## King, councils and Cortes*

The King's power within the Spanish Monarchy varied according
to regional tradition and custom. It was most extensive in Castile,
where he resided, maintained his court and the councils of government. The King was *absoluto*; this meant he had no superior in
Castile. He was the source of all authority, made all appointments
and all the laws. In addition, he had complete control over policy
and 'could requisition property, demand personal services for
war, and exploit a wide, and imprecisely defined, range of regalian
rights over money, trade, land, offices, status and honours' (**110**,
p. 85). However, there was a lot of difference between the theory
of 'absolute royal power' and its practical application. In reality
there was a myriad of restrictions limiting the King's power.

The King was bound by the law. Moreover, law-making itself was
restricted by tradition and custom, and by the device whereby laws
were 'to be obeyed but not put into effect' (*obedézcase, pero no se
cumpla*) pending an appeal to the Council of Castile. The sheer
size of the Monarchy and its governmental problems created the
need for an extensive bureaucracy, and this too acted as a brake on
royal power, as did the Cortes*, which played an important role in
the imposition of taxation. The Church too could be an impedi-
ment, since the King required the approval of the Pope in Rome to
exercise his authority in its regard, and the clergy themselves often
'spearheaded resistance to taxation' (**110**, p. 83).

'The formality of the court, its clockwork routine, the privacy of
the royal person, the public impassivity of the king – Philip IV
was described by foreign visitors as like a statue – were part of a
propaganda of monarchy as an institution in which the office was
greater than the man' (**110**, p. 73). However, the personality of the
ruler remained of fundamental importance, and in the seventeenth century Spain was not blessed with outstanding monarchs.
Philip III (1598–1621) was a reluctant king; his son Philip IV
(1621–65), though infinitely more conscientious, was weak and

indecisive, and his son, Charles II (1665–1700), was retarded. More often than not, policy in the seventeenth century was decided by the councils or the ministers, or indeed by a single minister. The all-powerful minister or *valido*\* (favourite) was a new phenomenon in the seventeenth century (and not only in Spain); Lerma under Philip III and Olivares under Philip IV exercised enormous control over policy and patronage. Subsequent ministers like Don Luis de Haro, in power between 1643 and 1661, the Duke of Medinaceli (1680–85) and the Count of Oropesa (1685–91, 1698–99) are more correctly described as prime ministers since their powers were more restricted. Thus an unsatisfactory king could be compensated for by a capable minister and an efficient bureaucracy.

Since the King could not be present in all his dominions, their interests were served by representation on councils sitting in Madrid. There were twelve councils in all, the most important being the Council of State (*Estado*), formed in 1526, which dealt with foreign policy. Next came the Council of War (*Guerra*), formed in 1522, which dealt only with peninsular Spain and was very much an adjunct to the Council of State. There were seven superior or supreme councils which were independent of one another but under the supervision of the Council of State. The most important was the Council of Castile which dealt with the administrative and judicial affairs of Castile, and its president was the second person in the kingdom after the King. The Chamber (*Cámara*) of Castile became a permanent department of the Council of Castile from 1588 to deal with Church affairs and appointments and grants of privileges. The Council of the Indies (1524) was also important because of its wide range of competence over the administration of the New World and overseas trade. The Council of Aragon (1494) usually consisted of Aragonese personnel and liaised with the viceroys of Aragon, Valencia, Catalonia, Sardinia and the Balearics. The Council of the Inquisition had been set up in 1483 and had a large staff 'on the ground' to enforce policy. The Council of Italy (1555) administered the Italian states of Milan, Naples and Sicily. This had been the responsibility of Aragon, but the creation of a separate council indicated the importance of this area to the Monarchy. The Councils of Portugal (1582) and Flanders (1588) were set up, like that of Italy, to deal with the day-to-day correspondence to and from these places. In addition to these seven superior councils, there were three more: Finance (*Hacienda*, 1523), which was responsible to the Council of Castile; Military Orders (1489), which administered the three chivalric orders; and Crusade (1509), which administered the *cruzada* tax – though the last two were not of any great significance in the seventeenth century.

All councils met in the royal palace on a specified day; but because there was so much business various sub-committees (or *juntas**) had to be set up on an *ad hoc* basis. In meetings members would express opinions (*votos*) which were synthesized into a report or recommendation (*consulta**) that was sent to the King. A *consulta* could be the basis for a royal decree, and legislation was usually a joint activity between the King and his councils. 'Thus the "territorial" councils administered the royal sovereignty, as well as being consulted upon its operation, in the lands under its supervision' (**99**, p. 25). Conciliar government enjoyed a revival under Philip III, and during the course of his reign the councils appear to have functioned well. Olivares set out to reduce the power of the councils by the use of *juntas*, and he was largely successful. However, this led to ministerial tyranny and allowed no expression of alternative opinion. After Olivares, a balance re-emerged between the King, the chief minister, the councils and the grandees, but in the reign of Charles II the weaknesses of the conciliar system came to outweigh its strengths.

Of course there had always been weaknesses in the conciliar system. The councils could be slow at reaching a decision and they generated a mountain of paper. A lot of their business was in any case trivial, relating to appointments and appeals of a minor nature. By the time of Charles II the councils had become obsessed with their jurisdictions and status, and often spent their time discussing these matters rather than the business of government. In addition, they became bloated with time-servers and representatives of faction. Whereas in the reign of Philip III the councillors were largely capable, by the time of Charles II there was a distinct lack of competent personnel. More and more appointments were made by purchase or favour, and unqualified aristocrats whose only interest was financial gain came to dominate. The conciliar system needed to be properly managed; in the time of Charles II it was not.

The councils could be ignored by the King and ministers; indeed, this is how Olivares was able to undermine them. However, although the government might ignore the councils on specific issues, it could never afford to ignore the political elite represented on them. 'Royal authority was simply not transferable, on a

7

regular basis, to the local level without the informal machinery of affinity and clientage which linked the court aristocracy and the higher bureaucracy with the local elites' (**110**, p. 93). The central government operated through about eighty *corregidores* – chief magistrates in the towns – but these positions had often been given as rewards and the holders were not reliable. In half the country there were no *corregidores* at all as jurisdiction belonged to lay lords or the Church. Thus power in the localities resided with the local bosses – the *poderosos* – who increased their control over justice as well as government (**45**). It has been suggested recently (**70**) that the sale of jurisdictions necessitated by the crown's shortage of money did not necessarily lead to any reduction in power or revenue, as the newly autonomous towns proved to be intensely loyal, and efficient in tax collection. However, by the reign of Charles II most towns were no longer 'newly autonomous' and the breakdown of efficient central government led to a general increase in corruption and waste. This situation was not helped by the virtual abolition of the Cortes* in this reign.

The Cortes* of Castile was a very small body. Initially consisting of thirty-six deputies representing eighteen cities, this number rose to forty deputies representing twenty-two cities in the reign of Philip IV. The Cortes was the 'key to political obedience' (**110**, p. 74) since the great cities dominated the Castilian country-side. Obviously it was easy to 'influence' a small number of deputies since many looked upon their appointment as an opportunity to make a fortune. The master stroke was to give the deputies a share in the sums they voted – usually around 1.5 per cent (**22**), though in practice they took a great deal more. The Cortes had real power. By the reign of Philip III its deputies were responsible for 50 per cent of tax grants (especially the *millones**) and there could be no new taxes without the Cortes's consent. Philip IV's authoritarian minister Olivares found the Cortes an obstacle and by the end of the 1630s the crown had established control over the *millones*, and thereby broken the contractual basis of the relationship with the Cortes. Subsequently it was decided to bypass the institution altogether. 'Sporadically from 1643, and conclusively from 1667, it was directly to the Cortes's cities that the crown applied for consent to taxation' (**110**, p. 82). The decision not to convene the Cortes was taken in 1667 for three reasons. Firstly, it cost a lot of money to run (500,000 ducats* was one estimate); secondly, it would be unlikely to grant much new taxation; and thirdly – and most significantly – the deputies were expected to make political demands, which would challenge the authority of a weak government. The cities were untroubled by the demise of the Cortes since it meant no new taxation (**107**). But the freezing of tax rates at the 1664 level destroyed government credit and prevented borrowing.

What can we conclude about government in seventeenth-century Castile? What we witness is best summed up in the phrase 'maximum concentration of power at the summit and the minimum irradiation of that power downward' (**112**, p. 64). However, translating command into compliance was a general problem for early modern governments, which illustrated the paradox of absolute authority and limited power. Even a strong minister like Olivares was frustrated by the system: 'Sire', he told the King, 'no town councillor in Spain, no constable, no notary, no lord, no grandee, no squire, nobody who owns the sales-tax of a village, nobody who has a *juro** on it, nobody who has any property, nor any man of influence in the place he lives, pays taxes, and when I say nobody, I mean nobody' (quoted in **110**, p. 94). The best Olivares could hope for was to make an inefficient system work better, but in the second half of the seventeenth century there was a progressive deterioration of control. In the reign of Charles II 'the sense of a total breakdown of government and law and order pervading the documents...is overwhelming' (**110**, p. 89). Royal authority was increasingly curtailed by laxity, corruption, immunity. In short, weak government in Madrid made a bad system even worse. And while royal authority was not strong in the localities within Castile, the government had even less control outside, in Aragon, Naples and Flanders .

## Kingdoms and provinces

Without a modern civil service the King of Spain could only rule his inherited territories by working through the traditional structures and the traditional elites, the upper clergy, nobles and municipal oligarchs. Close control was impossible because of the distances involved. It took a minimum of two weeks for a letter from Madrid to reach Milan or Brussels, two months (minimum) to reach Mexico and a year to reach the Philippines (**74**). Even within the Iberian peninsula distances were considerable and communications poor.

The realms of the peninsula were divided by laws, customs barriers and languages. Even within the crown of Castile there existed the kingdom of Navarre with its own laws, Cortes*, coinage and customs posts. The King was represented by a viceroy (serving one or more three-year terms) but the realm was 'almost wholly independent' (**48**, p. 14). The Basque provinces (Vizcaya, Guipúzcoa and Alava) also had a considerable degree of independence. The crown of Aragon – which included the realms of Aragon, Catalonia, Valencia, the Balearic Islands and Sardinia – had its identity enshrined in highly developed *fueros**, or constitutional rights. Each of these realms was governed independently, each had its own laws and tax system, and in each the King was represented by a viceroy. Portugal had been independent until 1580 and was very loosely governed (**88**). Indeed, all the realms within the Iberian peninsula, excepting Castile, enjoyed a great deal of autonomy and contributed next to nothing to the running of the Monarchy. It was for this reason that Philip IV's minister Olivares made a dramatic attempt (see Chapter 4) to obtain men, money and matériel in a more coordinated way, yet he thereby drove both the Catalans and Portuguese into open rebellion in 1640. The Catalans were restored to allegiance and thereafter proved loyal and willing to pay tax. Portugal, on the other hand, re-established its independence.

Spain dominated Italy, for the King of Spain ruled in Sicily, Naples, Milan, the *presidios** and Sardinia, as well as dominating a whole host of princelings who were in receipt of annual pensions. Even a large state like Genoa was very much a satellite of Madrid. The traditional view used to be that Spanish government in Italy was oppressive and exploitative, but it seems this is in need of modification. For one thing, the viceroys were simply not as powerful as the criticism implied, and although they were concerned to maximize revenue, they also sought to retain allegiance by controlling grain prices and ensuring food supplies (**13, 65, 66**).

In Sardinia, the viceroy had to defer to the aristocracy of Spanish descent and the *Parlamento* that had some legislative rights. The power of the *Parlamento* was much greater in Sicily, where it was dominated by the aristocracy. Taxation could only be raised by consent and this prevented fiscal exploitation. In contrast to Sicily, the Spanish viceroy in Naples had a freer hand and could extract greater taxation and man-power. Fiscal exploitation led to a serious rebellion in 1647; after it was overcome taxation was lessened, but the devastating plague of 1656 ensured that Naples could not be exploited thereafter. On the whole Spain did rather well out of Naples in the first half of the seventeenth century; it was a great source of both revenue and man-power. Milan had much more autonomy. Though the governor was always a Spaniard – his responsibilities as commander of the army of Lombardy, second in size to that of Flanders, made this essential – his powers were quite limited. Undoubtedly Milan's strategic position engendered a cautious approach by Madrid (**87**).

Spain also appointed governors to rule in the Burgundian terri-tories of Franche-Comté and Flanders. The looseness of Spanish rule in Franche-Comté ensured a loyalty which endured long after the country had been conquered by Louis XIV. Flanders – the name most commonly given to the Spanish Netherlands – was ruled from Brussels and the governorship here was possibly the most important appointment in the Spanish Monarchy, since the Army of Flanders was Spain's largest fighting force. At the end of the sixteenth century Philip II had given sovereign control (in reality, domestic autonomy) to his daughter the Archduchess Isabella and her husband the Archduke Albert, known collectively as the Archdukes. With the death of Albert in 1621 and Isabella in 1633 full sovereignty reverted to King Philip IV, but the impor-tance of this area was recognized by the appointment of his brother, the Cardinal Infante Ferdinand, as governor (1635–41). He was succeeded by the Emperor's brother Leopold William (1647–55) and Philip's own illegitimate son Don Juan José (1656–59). Communications with Flanders were a perennial problem; the land route, the Spanish Road*, was closed for good in the 1630s, as was the sea route after 1639. After 1659 the Army of Flanders was run down and the defence of this area came to rest largely with the Dutch and the Emperor. In the last forty years of the century Spanish control of Flanders was virtually non-existent, yet the alternative, harsh French rule ensured a remarkable continuing loyalty to Madrid.

Control was much more substantial in the Spanish Indies where viceroys for Mexico and Peru had been appointed since 1535. America was ruled directly by Castile through the Council of the Indies, and Madrid had supreme control over all administrative, judicial and ecclesiastical matters. In America itself the two viceroys had to devolve power to subordinate governors who enjoyed enormous influence by virtue of their remoteness from the metropolis. The power of the viceroy was balanced by the *audiencias*\* which kept an eye on them and had administrative as well as judicial functions. Naturally as time passed the colonial aristocracy developed their own interests unchecked by interference from Madrid, but under Olivares the New World was subject to greater taxation and bureaucratic efficiency.

Overall, what is striking about the kingdoms and provinces of the Spanish Monarchy is that cooperation was the norm and rebellion was rare. However, we cannot escape the conclusion that Spanish control was tolerated largely because it was so loose. Spain ruled through the local elites and they benefited from Madrid's patronage and their control in the localities; there was no better alternative for them. When greater fiscal exploitation and greater government control were attempted, as under Olivares, this could rapidly lead to a breakdown. The viceroys did not have substantial forces at their disposal; they relied entirely on the local barons who could withdraw their goodwill at any time. Generally, the local elites were not prepared to finance substantial defence forces, which is why the bulk of the cost of the Monarchy had to be met by Castile.

## Finance

Defence was of course the principal item of expenditure in the Monarchy's budget, but expenditure was largely determined by policy interests rather than by income. Of course, if the money could not be found, a policy might have to be curtailed and a campaign cancelled; but usually expenditure was met by borrowing and the alienation of future revenues. In the reign of Philip III (1598–1621) expenditure was probably around 8–10 million ducats* per annum, but it rose to 12 million in the reign of Philip IV (1621–65) [doc. 1]. By the end of Philip's reign and throughout Charles's reign expenditure was severely restricted by debt payments and reduced income.

The largest item in the budget in the first half of the century was usually the Army of Flanders. This cost about 4 million ducats* per annum, and even during the Truce (1609–21) expenditure was in the region of 1.5 million ducats annually. In the 1640s expenditure probably halved (to 2 million) and after 1656 it declined dramatically; in the budget of 1690 there was no provision at all [doc. 2]. The Army of Milan was usually funded in Italy itself but in the reign of Philip IV large amounts of money were sent annually from Madrid; for example, 2.5 million ducats in 1637. In Charles II's reign it was funded entirely in Italy once again. Fighting within the peninsula (with France in the late 1630s and with Catalonia

1640–52 and Portugal 1640–68) no doubt accounts for the reduction in funds to Flanders and Milan in the 1640s. In 1644, 1.6 million ducats were spent on the army in Spain, up to 2.5 million in 1646; at the end of the reign, Philip IV was spending about 5 million ducats annually on the war with Portugal.

Naval expenditure regularly ran to between 1 and 1.5 million ducats* annually, divided roughly equally between the Atlantic (galleon) and the Mediterranean (galley) fleets. However, after the destruction of the Atlantic fleet in the battle of the Downs (1639) expenditure declined and the lost ships were not replaced. Similarly, after the destruction of the Mediterranean fleet in 1676, there was no attempt to make good the losses.

Philip III was quite an extravagant king and his household expenses reached about 1.3 million ducats* annually. This was reduced in Philip IV's reign to about 600,000 ducats per annum (about 5 per cent of expenditure). However, in the reign of Charles II household expenditure rocketed again to about 1.5 million in 1690, reflecting not only the existence of three royal households (the King, the Queen and the Queen Mother) but the profligacy of a faction-ridden court.

What were the sources of government revenue in Castile? First of all there were the customs duties and the *alcabala*. The latter was nominally a 10 per-cent sales tax, often paid in the form of a lump sum by the cities. By 1612 it was yielding 2.75 million ducats* but its potential was limited by ecclesiastical immunity and the increasing sale of collection for a lump sum to private individuals. The *servicio*\* (apportioned among households) was granted by the Cortes\* and was fixed at 405,000 ducats. By far the most important grant, however, was the *millones*\*, a tax on basic foodstuffs (meat, wine, oil and vinegar) which yielded 2–3 million ducats per annum. In addition, the crown had revenues from ecclesiastical sources which were granted by the Pope as a matter of course. The 'Three Graces', as they were known, were the *cruzada* (the sale of indulgences) which yielded in excess of 800,000 ducats; the *subsidio* (from Church revenues) yielding 420,000 ducats; and the *excusado* (from the tithe) about 250,000 ducats per annum. The crown also possessed its celebrated revenue from the Indies which yielded about 2 million ducats in 1600 (but was down to less than half that by 1620 and half again by 1650). These figures relate to the reign of Philip III; in the first half of Philip IV's reign the grants from the Cortes\* of Castile provided about 38 per cent of revenue, the 'Three Graces' 15 per cent, and bullion about 9.5 per cent. In addition, the government made a substantial sum (9 per cent of revenue 1621–40) on the sale of (and discounts on) *juros**. A *juro* was a contract whereby a person or institution gave a lump sum to the crown and received in return an annual pension charged on a specific revenue. This then became a piece of property which could be inherited or traded. The *juro* was the principal debt of the Monarchy (see below). Another significant source of income (7.5 per cent in 1621–40) was the manipulation of the coinage, a process started by Lerma with the debasement of *vellón**. It has been calculated that currency manipulation generated greater income than the silver from the Indies! In the reigns of Philip IV and Charles II the government also resorted to *donativos**; these were in theory benevolences from those best able to pay, a sort of voluntary contribution, but in practice the government had to grant privileges to make them a success. They were irregular and unpredictable but yielded about 5.5 per cent of revenue in 1621–40. Their frequency in the reign of Charles II reduced their efficacy. Under Olivares a number of new taxes were introduced; in 1631 the *lanzas* (cash instead of military service), the *media anata** ('half year' of income from all official posts), and the salt tax (soon dropped). In 1636, a stamp tax on documents (*papel sellado*) as well as a tax on playing cards were introduced. In addition, the government made money from the sales of offices and jurisdictions (3.5 per cent of revenue 1621–40) and by taxing *juros* (in effect discounting the pay-out).

Although we can identify sources of revenue, it is extremely difficult to determine actual revenue. In the reign of Philip III income was probably around 8–10 million ducats* per annum, about 50 per cent of which was voted by the Cortes*. During Philip IV's reign the yield from directly levied taxes probably more than doubled, but the crown never received all it was entitled to. Local authorities and middlemen who were responsible for collecting the taxes kept a substantial portion for themselves. A memorial of 1655 claimed that only 5.5 million out of 14 millions of *servicios** were reaching the King (**106**, p. 31, n. 9). 'Fraud and evasion became more common as the state's demands became more pressing and its administration less efficient, as it did towards the end of Philip IV's reign' (**63**, p. 111) and throughout the reign of Charles II. In fact the dramatic expansion of taxation in the reign of Philip IV created spectacular opportunities for the middlemen – bankers, military entrepreneurs, strategically placed ministers and royal officials, tax collectors, the administrators of royal rents, and the *poderosos* of the towns and villages – to grow rich. In the mid-1640s the Council of Castile reported that the 'number of tax collectors who eat up Your Majesty's kingdoms now exceeds 20,000' (quoted in **95**, p. 127). During the 1650s Philip IV's government wrested the *millones*\* from municipal control, but this advance was short-lived as the weak Regency government of Mariana gave them up in 1669 (**107**). In Charles's reign (1665–1700) the situation got even worse and revenue actually declined to about 8 million ducats.

Throughout the seventeenth century the Spanish Monarchy was saddled with an ever-increasing cumulative *juro*\* debt. This was about 85 million ducats\* in 1598, and meant that about 4.5 million ducats annually had to be taken out of income and assigned to the payment of *juros*. By 1623 the debt stood at 112 million ducats, requiring 5.5 million to be assigned; the annual requirement was 6.4 million in 1637 and was held down by discounts and suspensions. However, with the succession of bankruptcies in the 1660s the requirement rose to 9 million on a debt of 221 million ducats in 1667. By 1687 the assignment was 12.2 million on an income of 8.4 (**21**).

How had this come about? Basically because the government's income did not meet its expenditure. Let us take for an example the 1640s, when 12 million ducats\* were needed for defence. Tax revenue should have yielded around 20 million; but after collection the government received only about 12 million. However, half of that had to be assigned to the cumulative *juro*\* debt; hence the government had to borrow 6 million to make up the shortfall. The government did this by selling yet more *juros*. However, the greatest expenditure occurred outside Spain, and international bankers (mainly Genoese) were needed to finance this. A contract (*asiento*\*) would be agreed in Spain for the banker to advance cash elsewhere: he in turn would issue 'bills of exchange' to be paid by a colleague abroad; the sum paid back to him by the government would include a fee – an interest payment of, say, 30 per cent – for the transaction (**52**). Clearly, there were occasions when the crown's anticipations and short-term debt commitments left it with very little free revenue. On these occasions the government would declare a 'bankruptcy': that is, a suspension of payments. In effect it turned short-term debts into long-term ones by paying the bankers *juros* which they then passed on to their creditors. This occurred in 1607, 1627 (when Olivares skilfully brought about 60 Portuguese bankers into the system) and 1647 (when the

15

Portuguese were driven out of business). The bankruptcies of 1652, 1660 (partial), 1662 and 1666 undermined the whole system of *asientos*. The few bankers who remained confined themselves to furnishing small sums at high rates of interest. The constant tampering with the *juros* and the inability to raise new taxes reduced government credit to nothing in Charles II's reign. His government resorted to *donativos** and the forced sale of *juros*, but by this time Spain was truly bankrupt.

What then are we to make of the Spanish government's finances? Clearly, it spent way beyond its means. Philip II had saddled the Monarchy with a colossal debt and Spain was caught up in the spiral of ever-increasing borrowing, mortgaging the future to pay for today. Throughout the seventeenth century the debt grew at an average of over 2 million ducats* per annum. Spain, or rather Castile, needed retrenchment and reform, for it has been estimated that in 1616 Castile was contributing about 75 per cent of the Monarchy's total costs. Within the Iberian peninsula the other kingdoms made a quite negligible contribution [**doc. 3**]. Between 1621 and 1640 Aragon only contributed 1.1 per cent to the overall income of the Monarchy. It was Olivares's achievement that he was able to persuade Aragon, Valencia and the Balearics to contribute more, but his efforts had disastrous consequences in Catalonia and Portugal. In America too he was successful in persuading the viceroyalties to contribute more to their own defence, but the Spanish Netherlands were a more sensitive area. Flanders paid a subsidy (*subsidio ordinario*) which was enough to pay for local administration and an army of about 15,000 but this was sufficient only for peacetime garrisoning. Extraordinary subsidies trebled in the 1620s (**40**) but there was no serious expectation that Flanders could support the army (which reached 90,000 in 1640), and strategic considerations prevented fiscal pressure reaching dangerous proportions (**63, 71**). The situation was similar in Milan where again strategic considerations rendered excessive tax demands inappropriate. The Army of Milan was mainly financed by loans (taken out by the Milanese government) and external subsidies, principally from Naples and Sicily (**87**) [**doc. 4**]. Indeed after Castile, Naples and Sicily contributed the greatest proportion to the Monarchy's defence. Beginning in the 1620s – as a temporary measure to make up for the shortfall in bullion – taxation increased dramatically, and during the viceroyalty of Medina de las Torres (1637–44), Naples provided the huge total of 3.5 million *escudos** annually. Over 1 million ducats were sent to Milan (**18**); other moneys were sent to Genoa and Germany. The remainder was spent within the kingdom on garrisons, fortifications and principally the galley fleet (**114**). But as in Castile this vast increase in expenditure could not be met by increased taxes alone; it also entailed anticipations, the sale of offices and jurisdictions, and a dramatic increase in borrowing. This in turn required greater taxation, which led to the revolt of 1647. Medina may have been an effective viceroy from Spain's point of view but he had brought the kingdom close to financial collapse. After 1647 taxation had to be reduced, and following the devastating plague of 1656 Naples could no longer make a significant contribution to the Monarchy. Sicily was more insulated from the demands of Olivares. The privileges of its two principal cities, Palermo and Messina, and the power of its *Parlamento* meant that the Spanish viceroy, the Duke of Alcalá, found it impossible to meet Olivares's requirement of an extra 1 million *escudos* a year. It was met by his successor, Francisco de Melo, in the late 1630s, but he warned of the dangers of continuing at this rate, and his warnings came true in the revolt of 1647 (**99**).

Indeed, although Olivares was successful in spreading the financial burden throughout the Monarchy, the outcome was revolt and rebellion (in 1640 and 1647), and the long-term consequence was a relaxation of political and fiscal pressure. His attempts at reform within Castile met with more immediate failure because of opposition from the Cortes*, and he was forced thereby to resort to fiscal devices that made a bad system worse. Important parts of royal administration and royal justice were sold off to the cities, nobles and provinces, and the sale of jurisdictions sometimes included taxation as well. Financial decentralization turned out to be a disaster, for the further the government got from the taxpayer, the further it got from the tax. Indeed, a good case could be made to suggest that the main problem facing the Monarchy was its unsatisfactory method of tax collection. Had it been able to realize the large sums actually due (in theory as high as 29 million *escudos** in the 1660s), the government would have been able to meet its expenses.

One of the major problems facing both the central government and the localities was the growth in tax arrears. A lot of these seem to have been the result of genuine hardship; the years 1647 to 1652 were particularly difficult. Many people simply could not pay (**80**). However, at some stage 'could not pay' must have turned into 'would not pay', and the weak government of Charles II afforded taxpayers the opportunity to plead poverty when it might not have been genuine. In 1688 the government tried to resolve the matter; it wiped the slate clean by cancelling all arrears. Nevertheless, the problem persisted and by the end of Charles II's reign there seems little doubt that Castilians were not paying as much tax as they could afford.

'The failure of the revenues was primarily a failure of control' (**110**, p. 90) and under Charles II's weak government revenue actually declined. Reforms were ineffectual and the government was too weak to impose new taxes. In exposing this weakness, however, we must not lose sight of the fundamental problem. Both Philip II and Philip IV took on commitments beyond the resources of the Monarchy. Only during the reign of Philip III under the direction of the Duke of Lerma was anything like a realistic policy adopted (see Chapter 3). By the time of the Regency (1665) Spain was prostrate, weighed down by a colossal debt. Weak government during the King's majority (from 1675) prevented a recovery.

## Military organization

If government was inefficient in tapping its financial resources, was it any better in military matters? The answer would appear to be a tentative 'yes'. Here, it seems, the same processes were at work – privatization and devolution – but they were more beneficial. After 1618 the government abandoned direct administration of all branches of military organization and 'by the 1630s practically the whole of the war machine, the high-seas fleets, the arms industries, the victualling of the galleys and African garrisons, and the recruiting process had passed into private hands, contracted out to entrepreneurs and local authorities' (**104**, p. 7; **81**).

The localization of administration – local authorities were by 1625 responsible for the militia and the nobles were required to serve and provide troops – reinforced the authority of the local elites and was therefore a fundamentally conservative policy. Contracting, on the other hand, was not, since it worked to the advantage of less-established social groups. Private contractors were usually foreigners, Genoese or Portuguese, and they were contracted to recruit soldiers overseas, supply the armies and provide the fleet. There is no doubt that contracting was a reflection of the inability of both the crown and Spanish business to mobilize capital for military investment and of Spanish agriculture and manufacturing to maintain military supplies, but as long as the crown had the money, the system worked well. By the 1630s the number of soldiers in the pay of Spain probably exceeded 170,000; and in 1638 the King could tell the Council of Castile that naval power had never been greater 'and this assertion may well have been correct' (**29**, p. 508). 'Taking the balance of evidence as a whole contracting as a practical alternative was certainly no worse than the malfunctioning administration it replaced, and it was often a considerable improvement. The fleets and garrisons were undoubtedly better paid, better fed, better armed and better equipped by good contracts than by bad *administración*' (**104**, p. 270). Spanish expenditure on the Army of Flanders was less in the period 1621–30 than either 1591–1600 or 1601–10 and yet the army size was greater – and better conditions and financial support also led to a sharp reduction in mutinies (**71**).

The disposition of Spanish forces – fleets in the Atlantic and the Mediterranean, and armies in Milan and Flanders – reflected the Monarchy's principal strategic concerns. The main function of the Atlantic galleon fleet was the protection of the transatlantic routes, for America was a great source of wealth both in terms of bullion shipments* and general commerce. The galley fleet, on the other hand, attempted to control the western Mediterranean, which was essential to maintain links with the Balèaric Isles, Sardinia and Italy. Italy was a great source of wealth, providing man-power, armaments, banking and naval resources, and the Army of Milan maintained Spanish dominance in the peninsula. Italy also served as a link to Spain's Burgundian territories. These were by far the most problematical for the Monarchy not only because they were distant but also because of their proximity to potential enemies, England and France, and because of the Dutch rebellion. For these reasons the Army of Flanders was Spain's principal army. Thus the main military forces of the Monarchy were placed well away from Spain. Spain itself was given relatively little protection, until it experienced invasion and rebellion in the third and fourth decades of the century.

The Army of Flanders was recruited from six 'nations': Spain, Burgundy, Italy, Germany (Habsburg lands), Flanders itself and Britain. Only the last-mentioned were not 'serving their prince'; the remainder were subjects of the Spanish Monarchy. The Spanish contingent was fairly small (10–15 per cent) but it was reckoned to be the backbone. The army peaked at around 90,000 men in 1640 [**doc. 5**], but about a third of this number could be tied down in garrison duty. The bulk of recruitment was undertaken in the locality; however, the Spanish and Italian contingents came via the Spanish Road* (see Map 2). They took ship from Spain and Naples to Genoa where they went overland to Flanders. The original route via Savoy was last used in 1620, since it was felt to be too close to a revived France. It was replaced by a route via the Valtelline and Alsace, until this too was cut off in 1631. Between 1631 and 1639 27,000 soldiers were sent by sea, but after the destruction of the Spanish Atlantic fleet in 1639 this was no longer really viable, though Spain still managed to transport silver for payment [**doc. 6**]. After 1640 numbers were reduced, but this was because priority was given to the Catalan front and troops were even ferried from Flanders to the Iberian peninsula. It is perhaps surprising that the Spanish Monarchy was unable to defeat the Dutch, but there were few pitched battles and most of the military activity consisted of siege warfare in which the defenders had the edge. In any event, the Dutch had the resources to match and even exceed the size of the Army of Flanders. After the peace with France in 1659 the army was run down and never really built up again. During the warfare of Charles II's reign Flanders was effectively cut off from Spain, and Madrid came to rely on the Dutch and the Emperor to defend the province. By the 1690s its forces were negligible and at the behest of the Dutch and Austrians both the governor and commander-in-chief were foreigners.

The Army of Milan consisted mainly of Spanish and Italian troops, the bulk coming from Naples; it peaked at about 40,000 in the 1630s and thereafter declined to about 10,000 in the 1660s. The devastation of Naples by the plague in 1656 deprived Milan of a valuable recruiting ground. As in Flanders, by the 1690s the Army of Milan was but a small contingent of a larger foreign force, Austrian in this case. During the second half of the century Spain's largest army came to be the one within its peninsula, usually fighting on the Catalan front. This army was built up to 20,000 by 1640 but rarely exceeded that figure. By the 1660s the government was having real difficulty in raising enough troops. On the Catalan front against the French in the 1670s, 1680s and 1690s about 26,000 were the most that could be raised, and often the number was much less.

The same pattern can be observed in the history of the navy in the seventeenth century. The Mediterranean galley fleet usually numbered about sixty vessels, of which the bulk were provided by Naples and Genoa. Spain was still in control of the western

Mediterranean as late as the 1640s (**19**), but thereafter was eclipsed by the Dutch, English and French. By the end of the century the fleet consisted of only a handful of vessels. The Atlantic galleon fleet consisted of the *Armada del Mar Océano* (forty vessels in 1622) based at Cadiz, Lisbon and Corunna, while about ten vessels were assigned to the *Armada de las Indias* to protect the silver fleets. Of great significance was the Flanders flotilla based at Dunkirk from the 1620s and consisting of about twenty-four vessels (plus privateers). Although the galleon fleet was substantial by the 1630s, it was spread too thinly to be a match for the Dutch. Moreover, when its power was concentrated in 1639 it suffered a massive defeat at their hands (the battle of the Downs) from which it never recovered. It is an irony that subsequently the Monarchy came to rely increasingly on Dutch naval power: by the 1660s the Dutch were escorting the silver fleets and in the 1670s the Dutch admiral de Ruyter gave his life in defence of Spanish Sicily. Spain never really succeeded in establishing a good regular navy (**50**).

## The economy

The Mediterranean had been the focus of sixteenth-century economic life, but in the seventeenth century it suffered agricultural depression, industrial and commercial decline and a drop in population. Castile had some 6.5 million inhabitants in 1600, but a decline set in after 1620 and by mid-century the figure was 4.5–5 million. Even by 1700 the population was less than it had been a century earlier. The kingdom of Aragon was fairly static at about 1.2–1.4 million. In contrast, Portugal experienced a slight increase over the century, moving up from a million to perhaps 1.2 million.

Castile was particularly hard hit by plague. Between 1596 and 1602 it suffered an actual decimation when 600,000 lives were lost; between 1647 and 1652 the plague probably carried off half a million (the population of Seville was halved in this outbreak), and between 1676 and 1685 perhaps another half million. It is impossible to put a figure on emigration and the impact of warfare, but these too took their toll. Recovery came after 1660 primarily in the coastal areas [**doc. 7**]. But recovery must be put in perspective; population levels had fallen so much that they were not regained until the middle of the eighteenth century. A similar pattern can be discerned in Spanish Italy. Sicily and Sardinia remained static throughout the century at around 1.1 million and 250,000 respectively. However, Milan declined; in the plague of 1630 fully one-third of the people died, reducing the numbers from about 1.2 million to 800,000 (**87**). In Naples there was a similar story; the plague of 1656 carried off 250,000 in the city (60 per cent of the inhabitants) and 27 per cent in the countryside (**66**). The population which had been 3 million in 1600 was only 2.5 million in 1700 (**72**). The Spanish Netherlands (at around 1 million) grew slightly, whereas Mexico and Peru doubled in the period 1570 to 1646 to 200,000 (the native Indian population, of course, declined dramatically).

The decline in the populations of both Castile and Naples, the most populous states of the Monarchy, is highly significant and of course had implications for the power of the Monarchy. Moreover, it would appear that plague was not the sole cause of decline; the poor climatic conditions of this period (which has been described as the 'little ice age') meant that agriculture could not support the existing levels of population (**74, 82**). In Castile, ten wet years from 1589 were followed, after a short respite, by ten years of drought up to 1614. Agricultural output slumped, and across the country the number of sheep fell by one-third (the depression in wool demand lasted from 1602 to 1686). This coincided with a massive increase in taxation. Peasants were forced to borrow, could not pay the debt back and either lost their holdings or remained on the land as leaseholders. The worst harvest of the century occurred in 1647, and although agriculture picked up in Catalonia and Valencia after 1650, Castile did not begin to recover until the 1680s.

A similar pattern can be discerned in Naples, where agricultural crisis began in the 1590s, and there was no recovery until the 1680s or 1690s (**2**). Harsh winters devastated the sheep stock – in 1611, 69 per cent were killed (several million), and in 1622, 67 per cent of those that were left (**66**)! Sheep farming did not pick up until the 1690s. The collapse of the economy used to be (erroneously) attributed to Spanish rule, but in fact the viceroy's government worked hard to balance the interests of agriculturalists and pastoralists, control prices and ensure food supplies. The situation was mirrored in Sicily: 1590–1610 were famine years and by 1630 exports of wheat were only one-third what they had been pre-1590 (though falling demand had much to do with this). In Milan too there was decline from 1620 but some recovery after 1660 with a shift to livestock. Unsurprisingly, the Spanish Netherlands again does not fit the Mediterranean pattern, for there was recovery after the low point of the 1580s, and yields were adequate although there was no advance.

In Castile, there was a dramatic decline in textile production, and in Milan too the urban textile industry declined. Remarkably, the silk industry in Sicily remained quite buoyant until the Messinese revolt in 1674. The Spanish Netherlands too were quite buoyant. Textiles here recovered and the diamond industry became established in Antwerp.

Castile had always had a massive trade deficit – importing manufactured goods and exporting raw materials (wool, wine and oil, mostly to America) – but this was paid for by the re-export of American silver. Indeed, Castile's control of the American trade made the country 'in some respects the greatest economic power on earth' (**42**, p. 189). By sealing off America, Spain had secured a vast captive market for silver, tobacco, dyes and so on. Together with Portugal, the Monarchy was able to dominate world trade routes, markets and resources. However, during the course of the seventeenth century the volume and value of the American trade fell, especially after 1620. By 1650, it was down 50 per cent. After 1650 the figures are incomplete and there was much contraband trade, but decline continued. The fundamental reason for the decline was that the colonies themselves were absorbing more of their own revenue in administration and defence costs. Warfare also affected commerce (particularly in 1629–31 and 1639–41) but embargoes on enemy commerce helped Spain to maintain its hold on the transatlantic trade (**42**, ch. 7). Paradoxically, it was peace and the concession of favourable terms to the Dutch (after 1648), the French (after 1659) and the English (after 1667) which led to foreign penetration. By the 1690s the trade out of Cadiz, which had largely replaced Seville during the second half of the century as the leading Spanish port, was dominated by the French, Genoese, Dutch and English (in that order); the Spanish only accounted for a meagre 5 per cent (**69**). Imports of bullion also slumped; they hit bottom in the 1650s [**doc. 8**] and although they subsequently made a considerable recovery, the government did not benefit, for its sequestrations of private bullion had led to massive evasion. Fraud became systematic, as the government of Charles II acknowledged by charging the occasional lump sum (*inducto*) as compensation. American silver never really played the dominant role that contemporary perception ascribed to it, but it was a source of ready cash and a means of credit. In Charles II's reign, when the government had no credit, it would have come in useful.

Mediterranean trade followed a similar pattern of native decline and foreign infiltration. The Dutch and the English had been called in to alleviate the grain shortage after 1590, and they stayed. By the second quarter of the seventeenth century cheaper English textiles were undermining native ones while low-cost Dutch shipping controlled the grain and timber trade. Naples and Sicily continued to export wheat, wool, wine and oil, but the availability of Baltic grain restricted the volume and what was exported was increasingly carried in foreign ships. The import of foreign manufactures resulted in a trade imbalance here too.

The economies of the Spanish Monarchy bear sufficient resemblance to one another to use the noun in the singular. A clear pattern emerges of severe recession, demographic loss, agricultural depression, industrial and commercial decline. The worst affected areas were the two most important kingdoms within the Monarchy, Castile and Naples. It is hardly surprising that the Spanish Monarchy experienced difficulties in raising revenue during the course of fifty years of warfare in such a deteriorating economic climate.

## Conclusion

Weak government and a deteriorating economy have to be placed in a relative context. With a population of about 15 million the Spanish Monarchy had enormous sources of power and strength, but fifty years of continual warfare (1618– 68), largely financed by only half the population (Castile and Naples), pushed Spanish resources and the structure of government to their limits. It is in contrast to the performance of other states that the Spanish Monarchy has to be judged, and here it is found wanting. France, with its compact geography, fertile agriculture and larger population (20 million), had a clear advantage over barren, depopulated Castile. But that said, it is clear the French were better able to tap their resources as time went on, whereas the Spanish became less so. Moreover, the growth in power of the small maritime states, England and the Dutch Republic, clearly demonstrated that a smaller population than that of France did not necessarily translate into dramatically inferior power. Spain's failure to progress had as much to do with weak government as with weak economic performance.

# Part Two:  Descriptive Analysis

## 3  The Reign of Philip III, 1598–1621

### King and *valido**

Philip II (1556–98) is traditionally regarded as a 'great' ruler, but he bequeathed his son a massive cumulative debt of 85 million ducats*, two wars to fight, and no money to wage them. Our view of Philip III is coloured not least by the judgment of his father: 'God who has given me so many kingdoms, has denied me a son capable of ruling them' (quoted in **61**, p. 14). It does not take much insight to guess at the psychological impact of the father's opinion on his son. Moreover, Philip II seems to have made no effort to introduce the young prince to the workings of government. Yet once his dominating father had died, Philip III set out to assert himself. He rejected many of his father's advisers, gave greater initiative to ministers and restored conciliar government (see Chapter 2). He re-established the power of the Council of State and he revived the other councils by appointing new members and encouraging their collaboration in government. This delegation of business was more realistic than Philip II's attempts to do everything himself and reflected the increasing importance of the bureaucracy. There is evidence that Philip III was very much part of government in this early phase, but after this initial flurry of youthful enthusiasm his commitment declined. He was not interested in the day-to-day running of the administration and he showed little interest in paperwork; even in the field of foreign affairs he endorsed without comment about 90 per cent of the recommendations of the Council of State (**74**).

'Travelling about one's kingdom is neither useful nor decent,' wrote Philip II to his son (**73**, p. 24), yet as if in wilful defiance of his father Philip III spent a great deal of time doing just that. His days were occupied by hunting, the theatre and lavish court fiestas, and he was notoriously extravagant. When he was not hunting he went on pilgrimages to sites of religious significance, many of them quite remote. These long *jornadas** that he undertook (in 1610 he spent nine months touring the hunting spots and local shrines of

Old Castile) were organized by the Duke of Lerma. Whether or not this absenteeism represented an 'escape from kingship' (**116**) is a moot point, since a quorum of the Council of State always accompanied Philip, and all the important decisions had to be taken by him. Philip ceased to travel around so much after 1611, and following the dismissal of Lerma in 1618 he resolved to act as his own first minister, so that 'papers shall be signed by me and no other person' (quoted in **52**, p. 201). Whether or not Philip III after Lerma would have developed into more of an independent working monarch is unanswerable since he died unexpectedly at the age of 42 in 1621.

While Philip III cannot now be accused of a total abdication of authority, there was nevertheless a total delegation of responsibility. Power was handed over to the Duke of Lerma [**doc. 9**]. Don Francisco Gómez de Sandoval y Rojas, the fifth Marquis of Denia and the first Duke of Lerma (1553–1625), was the first minister of the crown in all but name and derived his power from his position as the *valido** – the royal favourite. This was formally legitimized in 1612 by a royal decree to the effect that orders by the Duke carried as much authority as if they had been personally issued by the King himself (**24**). Lerma has had a bad press. Too often his administration has been viewed through the distorting lens subsequently applied to it by the Olivares faction (**29**, **115**). Moreover, his preference for governing through the spoken rather than the written word makes him a difficult subject to study. Although he was a member of the Council of State, he rarely attended meetings – 22 out of a total of 739 (**61**) – preferring to exercise power from behind the scenes. Historians have to some extent equated the absence of written evidence with indolence and have concentrated on Lerma's acquisition of wealth (by the end of the reign he had amassed a fortune in excess of 3 million ducats*) and the promotion of his family to positions of influence. There is no doubt that he was vain and derived much pleasure from power and the pomp that accompanied it; moreover, it is also true that he was bored by routine administration and left it to others. However, the more we learn of this first *valido* the more it seems he was thorough in consultation and conscientious in relaying information to the King. He was a kindly character and a good listener (**95**) and was deft at the exercise of patronage (**29**), operating through personal contact and oral instruction as a sort of godfather (**100**).

After the repression of the aristocratic factions at court by the reclusive Philip II and the atrophy of the councils in the 1580s and

1590s, there was bound to be a reaction. 'The premiership of the Duke of Lerma in the reign of Philip III was a manifestation of the recovery of political influence by the great aristocracy, or a section of them, and the councils, the Council of State in particular' (**110**, p. 87). The various councils seized the opportunity to formalize their routines and consolidate their areas of special jurisdiction; and as their business grew their secretariats multiplied. This growth of power could have represented a potential threat to Lerma but he made sure his extensive clientage system embraced the government as well as the court.

Given his indifference to the day-to-day routine of government Lerma was indeed fortunate that the personnel – the *letrados** – of government was in general highly competent. 'It so happened that the Monarchy never had better or more loyal servants' (**22**, p. 85). The name of Juan de Idiáquez stands out as the single most influential voice in the King's council (to his death in 1614). But while much of the business of government during the Lerma years devolved upon others, Lerma reserved for himself as many as possible of the major decisions that determined royal policy. Apart from Lerma there was little support for peace with England in 1604, and yet it happened. Again, in 1609 Lerma gained acceptance of the Truce of Antwerp with the Dutch in the face of considerable opposition. The expulsion of the Moriscos* and the general reorientation of policy towards an anti-Islamic Mediterranean stance must also be attributed to Lerma, as should the marriage alliance with France (negotiated from 1611). This was not an 'absence of foreign policy' (**52**, p. 206), but a radical reversion to the strictly Iberian interests of the Catholic Monarchs.

Lerma's power and influence were not uniform throughout Philip's reign. He survived the financial indiscretions of some of his clients in 1607 and even the removal of his main lieutenant, Rodrigo Calderón, in 1612 – although the royal confirmation of his position in 1612 may reflect the fact that his policy pronouncements had been called into question. Philip curtailed his travels significantly after the death of his beloved wife in 1611, and was now open to influence from other advisers, particularly his confessor, Fray Luis de Aliaga (**116, 117**). From this time Lerma's influence began to wane, albeit slowly. After 1615 it would appear that both faction and policy were moving against the Duke, yet he was not removed from office until 1618, and even so it would appear he retained the King's personal affection to the last. That he was able to hold power for so long must say something about his political ability.

## Las Paces

To describe Philip as 'peace-loving' (**22**, p. 32) does not accord with his early reign. On his accession he was anxious to continue the fight against England, and he stepped up the tempo of the war in Flanders. However, given the crown's dire financial position, this ambitious policy was wholly unrealistic and was quickly modified. In 1604 Lerma negotiated the Treaty of London, which put an end to the war with England. This left Philip free to concentrate on reducing the Dutch rebels. In 1600 the Army of Flanders was mauled at Nieuwpoort and the French occupied Savoy, thereby threatening the Spanish Road*, the link between Milan and Flanders (**71**). However, the main problems in these years were caused by troop mutinies due to a lack of money. Accordingly, Ambrosio Spinola, a member of a prominent Genoese banking family and a wealthy man in his own right, was sent at the head of 9,000 men to transform the situation. He captured Ostend in 1604, and was subsequently made commander-in-chief of the Spanish Army of Flanders, a position he would hold for over two decades. He went on the offensive in 1605 and in 1606 penetrated the Dutch defences. But at this point the money ran out and another mutiny occurred. Spain was in need of peace. The Dutch too, fearing Spinola's 1607 campaign, wanted a cessation of hostilities.

An intricate peace process began in 1606 and finally resulted in the signing of the Twelve Year Truce at Antwerp in April 1609 [**doc. 10**]. A full peace had been the original intention, but total agreement could not be reached. The Truce acknowledged Dutch independence, made no provision for the Dutch to withdraw from Spanish possessions in the East Indies and did not bring any concessions for Dutch Catholics or for Antwerp (the Scheldt continued to be blockaded). This was a humiliating set-back for Spain. It was greeted with shock and indignation in Madrid, and Lerma had to work very hard to get it accepted (**29**).

## The expulsion of the Moriscos*

Lerma was determined that the year 1609 should not be remembered for the Truce, but for something much more significant, an act which would purify the kingdoms. The Moriscos were the descendants of the Arab conquerors who had been converted to Christianity, hence their other name, New Christians. However, few conversions were genuine; the bulk remained Muslim and Arabic-speaking. The revolt in Granada between 1568 and 1571 had led to some dispersion but this had made matters worse by spreading the problem; the Moriscos did not integrate and their numbers grew, particularly in Aragon and Valencia. They were considered to be a state within the state and a genuine threat to security. In 1582 expulsion had been decided upon, but international events and opposition from the Valencian nobles postponed implementation. On 30 January 1608 the Council of State decided that the time was right.

Disengagement in northern Europe and psychological compensation for the humiliation of the Truce were obviously factors in this decision (**61**). But it is also true that the government viewed the Moriscos as a threat to the integrity and security of the Monarchy (**95**) and there was a genuine popular movement for expulsion (**24**). It was also very much part of Lerma's reorientation of Spanish foreign policy. The operation was carried out with remarkable efficiency. A regiment of veterans was brought over from Naples, galleys were assembled, and between 1609 and 1614 about 300,000 Moriscos were expelled. But the expulsion also had serious economic consequences as Valencia lost one-third of its population. Lerma followed up the operation with a series of successful amphibious assaults against the Barbary Coast and Malta.

## The *Pax Hispanica*

On 14 May 1610 a priest named Ravaillac assassinated King Henry IV of France, and for his (inadvertent) services to Spanish diplomacy he was tied to four horses and literally torn apart. This dramatic event signalled the beginning of a period of peace that is known as the *Pax Hispanica* (**111**). 'In the decade after 1610 Philip III seemed "monarch of the world", more powerful in peace than his father had been in war' (**111**, p. 269). Brilliant diplomacy raised 'Spanish influence to the highest point it ever achieved in Europe' (**52**, p. 206). Cárdenas in Paris, Gondomar in London, Bedmar in Venice, and Zúñiga and Oñate in Vienna by tireless work, pensions and flattery were able to ensure that Spanish power and interests were never ignored. The religious progress of the

Counter-Reformation also seemed to be merely another dimension of the Spanish advance in Europe, and Spanish culture became fashionable from London to Prague. As Ben Jonson put it in *The Alchemist* (1610):

> Your Spanish jennet is the best horse. Your Spanish
> Stoup is the best garb. Your Spanish beard
> Is the best cut. Your Spanish ruffs are the best
> Wear. Your Spanish Pavan the best dance...
> ... And as for your Spanish pike
> And Spanish blade, let your poor Captain speak.
>
> (quoted in **95**, p. 77)

However, the *Pax Hispanica* was really something of a 'sleight of hand' (**25**, p. 12; **29**, p. 52) since it depended above all upon the passivity of France. Henry IV had been preparing to challenge Spain in both the Rhineland and Italy, but his assassination gave Spain a chance to prolong its hegemony. The reluctance of the regency government of Marie de Medici to pursue a bellicose foreign policy was seized upon by Lerma as an opportunity for a *rapprochement* with France, and he proposed a dynastic alliance. This was agreed in 1611, the treaty was signed in 1612, and in 1615 the young Louis XIII married Anne of Austria (Philip III's daughter) while the young *príncipe* Philip was wedded to Elizabeth of France. A similar bait was held out to James I, and this ensured English co-operation for many years to come. At first sight the marriages were a triumph for the moderate and pacific policies with which the Duke of Lerma had come to be identified, and which, he believed, could maintain Spain's predominant position in Europe without loss to its reputation. But in practice the new friendship foundered as early as 1616 and thereafter reverted to characteristic mutual suspicion, despite Philip III's regular correspondence with his son-in-law. Only the domestic preoccupations of the French government prevented a confrontation (**29**).

In these years Lerma also undertook secret negotiations with the Dutch in order to turn the Truce into a full peace settlement, but little headway was made. Both Oldenbarnevelt and Lerma wanted a settlement, but the Dutch would not agree to evacuate the Far East, nor would Spain abandon its freedom of action in Europe. When Spanish troops seized Wesel in 1614 in support of the Catholic candidate in the second Cleves-Jülich crisis*, the atmosphere of mutual suspicion became intense.

## Zúñiga and war

Precisely how Lerma came to fall from power is not altogether clear, but opposition to him was nothing new. As we have seen, Lerma's conciliatory policy had always provoked criticism, particularly peace with England in 1604 and the Truce with the Dutch in 1609, which many considered a gross humiliation. However, towards the end of the reign criticism was rising to a crescendo, at a time when the peculation and unpopularity of the Duke's 'creatures' were bringing him into widespread disrepute. After 1612 he had less control over the King (**117**); he was now an old man (60 in 1613) and he constantly talked of retirement (though without actually retiring!). 'Activism' was gradually permeating the government, and in 1617 Spain made a secret agreement with the Archduke Ferdinand of Styria, recognizing him as heir to the Imperial title in return for the cession of some Austrian Habsburg possessions in Alsace, a key territory on the Spanish Road* (though they were never actually handed over). How far these changes represented flexibility by Lerma or his loss of control is debatable.

'If any one event can be said to mark the transition from the quiescent Lerma epoch to the new activism ... it was the return from Prague of Don Baltasar de Zúñiga to take up his seat on the Council of State in Madrid in July 1617' (**30**, p. 118). Zúñiga had been ambassador in Brussels (from 1599), Paris (from 1603) and in Vienna (from 1608). It can be no coincidence that Lerma had tried unsuccessfully to keep this strong personality away from Madrid by trying to send him as ambassador to Rome after Vienna. Zúñiga found natural allies in the influential Fray Luis de Aliaga, the King's confessor (since 1608), and Fray Juan de Santamaría, a royal chaplain. In 1615, Santamaría had published a book, *República y política cristiana*, which urged Philip to govern without a favourite and to invest his trust instead in ministers and councils (**117**). This may have had more impact than any 'rising tide of activism', for we know that Philip III read this book and that Santamaría stayed with him in the summer of 1618. Lerma was astute enough to realize that his position was deteriorating, and throughout 1617 he worked hard to obtain a Cardinalate which would provide him with immunity in his retirement. It appears that his dismissal may well have occurred at the time he became a Cardinal in March 1618 (**117**), but he lingered for a further six months and it needed a push from his son, the Duke of Uceda, to get him to leave in October 1618.

Prior to his departure Lerma tried to salvage a project dear to his heart: the dispatch of a major naval expedition to Algiers (11). But Zúñiga, convinced of the need to save the Emperor from the rising tide of heresy and subversion in the hereditary lands, called for aid to Vienna instead. When Oñate's news of the defenestration of Prague* arrived in Madrid in July 1618, it was decided to send 200,000 ducats* to assist the Emperor against the Bohemian rebels; a further 500,000 ducats were sent in September, by which time Lerma had clearly lost control of foreign policy.

History has not treated Lerma kindly. This is surprising, since with hindsight we can see that his peace policy (the Mediterranean excluded) was sensible and realistic given the Monarchy's limited resources. Referring to the intervention in Bohemia, he argued (correctly) that 'it would be impossible to find a way out' (July 1618). The momentous decisions of 1618 to 1621, which involved war in Germany and renewal of the conflict with the Dutch, inaugurated a period of warfare that lasted fifty years and put an overwhelming strain on an already fragile entity. Of course it was not the intention of the decision-makers of 1618–21 to take the Monarchy to the brink of disaster (the contrary, in fact), yet they were prepared to take risks that Lerma had been determined to avoid. Lerma believed 'that it would be enough to maintain the position already acquired, taking small defensive measures, with an occasional demonstration of power in order to preserve prestige' (**21** in **95**, p. 69). In essence it was a policy of *conservación**, and as such it was sober and realistic.

Zúñiga convinced the King that the Emperor could not be abandoned, 'for such a withdrawal of Your Majesty's protection would deprive him of all his reputation'. He also convinced the King that Spain's position in Italy very much depended on the survival of the House of Austria. Zúñiga's policy, then, was preventive; he had no wish to precipitate a general European conflict. In this he was supported by the Archduke Albert and Spinola in Brussels, who felt that a show of strength by intervention in Germany would help to prolong the Truce with the Dutch. The problem was that although Spanish moves were decided out of defensive considerations, to others they appeared provocative and lent credence to the idea that Spain aspired to universal monarchy.

Spanish intervention in the Empire was very successful. In 1619, after the death of the Emperor Matthias, 17,000 troops were sent to assist the Archduke Ferdinand, now Emperor Ferdinand II, against the rebels; and in the following year Spinola occupied the Rhine territories of Frederick of the Palatinate, whom the Bohemians had elected as their King. He thereby kept open a vital link in the Spanish Road*. In the same year the Duke of Feria secured the Valtelline*, another link in the chain of communications which effectively created a new Spanish Road. All this had been achieved without so far provoking a general war (**10, 11, 12**).

Despite Zúñiga's fervent belief in the need to assert Spanish power more vigorously, and his distaste for the Truce terms agreed in 1609, it would be wrong to assume that the Spanish leadership was firmly set on resuming the war with the Dutch Republic [**doc. 11**]. The strongest pressure for the resumption of the war came from the Councils of Portugal and the Indies. The massive Dutch incursion into the Indian and Pacific oceans not only represented a loss of trade and wealth to the Portuguese crown and Portuguese merchants, but also undermined the union of the crowns of Castile and Portugal. The Dutch had established forts in West Africa, India and Indonesia and even at the mouth of the Amazon, thereby threatening Portugal's Brazilian sugar trade. Moreover, the activities of Dutch merchants were subverting Castile's economy and its Atlantic trade, while Dutch intrigue was aiding Spain's enemies wherever they might be. In short, it was felt the Dutch had used the Truce to take advantage of the Spanish Monarchy [**doc. 11**].

In 1620 Don Carlos Coloma, the governor of Cambrai, complained: 'if the truce is continued, we shall condemn ourselves to suffer at once all the evils of peace and all the dangers of war' (quoted in **111**, p. 280). He argued for either a 'good peace' or a 'good war' (June 1620). In January 1621 the Council of State seems to have opted for a 'good war', but negotiations continued right up to the end of March to obtain a prolongation of the Truce on better terms. These included Dutch withdrawal from the Indies and the lifting of the Scheldt blockade. Failure to achieve these concessions, it was argued, would make peace more expensive than war. Thus for Spain the object of the struggle was not reconquest but reputation and economic well-being.

In fact the militancy of the Dutch in 1621 made the agonized debate in Madrid about terms and conditions almost wholly irrelevant. Oldenbarnevelt had fallen from power in 1618, and neither the Stadholder, Maurice of Nassau, nor the States-General were prepared to make concessions to Spain in order to extend the Truce. On the day of Philip III's death, 31 March 1621, the Archduke wrote to Madrid to report the failure of negotiations. On 9 April the Truce expired.

## The call for reform

The *Pax Hispanica* had done little to ameliorate Spain's financial difficulties, though no doubt a continuing war with the Dutch would have made matters worse. By 1617 proposed expenditure had risen to 12 million ducats*, while 'free' revenue (after debts) amounted to only 5 million; in 1618 'free' revenue dropped to 1.6 million. By 1621 revenue was anticipated up to 1625. There was a decline in bullion shipped from America in this period, since resources had to be redirected to the Philippines, and to make up for this, extra taxes were raised in Milan, Naples and Sicily. There was little prospect of raising extra taxes in Castile, for the decline in population which had set in about the 1580s and had been exacerbated by the plague of 1596–1602 naturally affected Castile's capacity to meet the fiscal demands of the crown. This paradox, that Spain, the greatest power in the world, should be so poor, led a growing number of clerics, lawyers, merchants, government officials (and cranks) to offer proposals to the government. These people were collectively, and pejoratively, known as *arbitristas** because they recommended *arbitrios* or expedients to the King.

The first flurry of writings appeared at the beginning of Philip III's reign between 1598 and 1605; they resumed with new intensity in 1614 and built up to a climax between 1617 and 1620 (**113**). The earlier treatises tended to look back to the reigns of Ferdinand and Isabella as a golden age, but as time passed and memories faded the later works tended to eulogize Philip II and criticize Philip III. Of the earlier writers the best-known was Martín González de Cellorigo whose *Memorial* appeared in 1600; he initiated the debate on the decline of Spain though it should be noted he was writing at the time of the plague [**doc. 12**]. The most significant of the later writers, apart from Santamaría, was Sancho de Moncada, whose *Political Restoration* appeared in 1619. He had studied the parish registers for the city of Toledo and noted that the number of marriages had declined by 50 per cent. He concluded that the reason for this was poverty: 'people no longer get married because they have no money to buy food and set up house together', he suggested, adding that the weight of taxes kept down the standard of living (**29**, p. 94; **113**). Indeed, many of the writers made correct assessments of Castile's economic problems – the *rentier* mentality, the neglect of the mechanical arts, the lack of productive investment, the weakness of the agricultural sector, the export of raw materials, the decay of native industries. Proposed solutions ranged from a reformation of manners and morals to a more equitable tax system and less profligacy in government (a swipe not only at Lerma's corrupt regime but at the King's own personal extravagance). In 1617 the government also found itself under attack from the Cortes* of Castile, and Lerma responded by setting up a *Junta* de Reformación* and asking the Council of Castile to find a remedy. On 1 February 1619 the council produced its famous reform *consulta**. This document identified the main problem as depopulation, which it attributed to the excessive burden of taxation. It proposed that the King should cut down on his liberal distribution of pensions, offices and honours, and argued that sumptuary legislation was essential for reform of manners and morals. Needless to say little was done; indeed, it remains an enduring criticism of the reign of Philip III and the Lerma regime in particular that the opportunity for reform was missed.

Of course, many of the *arbitristas** understandably only criticized what they saw in front of them, the corruption at court, the poverty in the countryside. What most of them lacked was a global perspective (Lope de Deza and Moncada are notable exceptions), for the real source of Castile's ills was the cost of defending such a large, far-flung set of territories. It was military expenditure that was draining Castile of its life blood, not pensions and favours. Avoiding large-scale military expenditure was the key to financial equilibrium, not the closure of brothels or the abolition of the ruff. However, as in all monarchies, foreign-policy decisions usually took precedence over financial considerations. A policy was decided upon in terms of Spanish interests, not cost; the funds had to be found afterwards. This is most clearly illustrated by the forward policy adopted between 1618 and 1621 when the finances were in such a parlous state.

The reign of Philip III has been the victim of a form of Whig history*. Historians in the past were inclined to identify the decline of Spain, because we know it happened, long before it did happen, and traditionally 1598 was their starting point. However, the Spanish Monarchy appeared far stronger at the death of Philip III in 1621 than at the death of Philip II (**74**). None of those who argued for military action in the period 1618–21 could have foreseen, for all their pessimism about the future, that this decision would lead to fifty years of war and put the entire Monarchy in jeopardy.

# 4   The Reign of Philip IV, (1) 1621–43

## Olivares

Philip IV was only 16 when his father died, and it is hardly surprising that at that age he did not fully take over the reins of power. But historians obsessed with the concept of long-term Spanish decline have depicted him in unflattering terms. One recent judgment is that 'his accession was accompanied by his virtual abdication' (**61**, p. 67)! In fact, Philip developed into quite a hard-working monarch (**1**), particularly after his illness in 1627, which he interpreted as a sign of God's dissatisfaction with his lack of application. Subsequently it appears he spent about six hours a day on his paperwork (**96**). He was reasonably intelligent, something of a scholar (between 1628 and 1633 he undertook a massive six-volume translation of Guicciardini's *History of Italy*) and a patron of the arts (he loved the theatre and became a great collector of paintings) (**99**). However, though more intelligent and hard-working than his father, Philip IV suffered from the same lack of self confidence (**25**, p. 28). He was nervous, weak-willed and, as the Flemish painter Peter Paul Rubens put it, 'defers too much to others' [**doc. 17**]. In any event, the amount of paperwork that the Spanish bureaucracy generated was enough to overwhelm any monarch, no matter how assiduous he might be in his duty. It is not surprising, then, that the King was happy to have a minister whose capacity for work appeared to be boundless. That minister was Olivares.

Gaspar de Guzmán, Count of Olivares (1587–1645), was from a junior branch of an illustrious family. He was born in Rome, grew up in Sicily and Naples (his father was viceroy in both), was educated at the University of Salamanca and spent his early manhood in Seville. He joined the future Philip IV's household in 1615 and, by encouraging the young prince's interest in riding and the theatre, was able 'to win a commanding position in his entourage' (**29**, p. 30). From 1617, with his uncle Zúñiga coming to dominate the Council of State, Olivares's star was in the ascendant. The early death of Philip III in 1621 was his opportunity. The Sandoval faction, Lerma's family and creatures, were now pushed out and replaced by those of the Zúñiga-Guzmán-Haro faction (Olivares's mother and wife were Zúñigas; his sisters married into the Haro family). Uceda was removed and placed in prison, where he died; Calderón was executed in August 1621; and Lerma himself, though he died of old age in 1625, was divested of much of his fortune. Olivares immediately (in April 1621) became Groom of the Stole and a grandee, and in December 1622 Master of the Horse. Although to some extent ceremonial, these positions were the key to Olivares's political control of the King, for they enabled him to live in the royal palace and have direct access to the monarch at all times. Although Olivares's influence grew, government policy remained in the hands of his experienced uncle until he died unexpectedly in October 1622. Zúñiga had a considerable impact on his nephew, and the policy aims he developed during these years – a strong link with Vienna, an improvement on the Truce terms with the Dutch, but above all the restoration of reputation – were to be inflexibly adopted by Olivares. Indeed, he would be governed by them throughout his long ministerial career.

On the death of his uncle Olivares joined the Council of State and became a minister for the first time. The British ambassador observed in December 1622 that Olivares was 'as absolute with this king as the Duke of Lerma was with his father' (quoted in **28**, p. 40). He was in fact the new *valido**, even though he was supposed to be opposed to that form of government. However, the Olivares regime took time to create, for he was little known and clearly had to establish his position. In order to increase his influence he set out to people the system with his 'creatures', adopting the same methods of patronage as the Duke of Lerma whom he so despised. He ensured that family and friends were placed in positions of importance in both the royal household and government, and he distributed jobs and titles to win allegiance. He also bypassed the councils where possible by creating *juntas**, small groups of hand-picked advisers – men whom Olivares could control and trust – and gradually emasculated the councils by leaving their presidencies vacant; these were also stratagems that had been employed by Lerma (**99**). The key to his position, of course, was his relationship with the King. It was a partnership, but Olivares was the senior partner and the relationship was akin to that of teacher and pupil; this was also reflected in their age difference of eighteen years. Olivares, who became the Duke of San Lúcar la Mayor in 1625 and was thereafter known as the Count-Duke, steadily increased his power throughout the 1620s, and despite the policy failures of 1628–31, he emerged in the 1630s with even greater power than before. It took monumental disasters and signs of instability before the King finally broke the umbilical cord in 1643.

Leaving aside his corpulence, Olivares is still not a very attractive figure; he was ruthless, impatient, aggressive, frequently rude, moody and inflexible (**5, 29, 61**). However, he had an enormous capacity for hard work, he was never lost for ideas (though he was not a clear thinker), and his industry, energy and intellect commanded awe and respect. He had a grandiose vision of Spanish power and a susceptibility to a wide range of reforming ideas which prompted a diplomat to comment perceptively that he was 'very inclined to novelties, without taking account of where they may lead him' (quoted in **52**, p. 211). It was widely felt by contemporaries that many of his schemes were not rooted in reality and this is why he failed both as a reformer and in his attempt to maintain Spain's *reputación** abroad. And yet he has been described as 'very nearly a great man' (**8**). Did he fail by a 'hair's breadth' or did he himself bring about Spain's demise?

## Reform

One of Olivares's more perceptive remarks (made in 1628) was that 'it would be better if many things were not as they are, but to change them would be worse' (quoted in **28**, p. 25), and indeed the whole experience of the Count-Duke's term of office suggests that reforms were easier to plan than implement. There was an inherent contradiction in trying to reform at a time of war, since *reputación** and *reformación* were not good bedfellows. For Olivares as well as Zúñiga the primary concern was the preservation of Spain as a world power. Reform was seen as a means to this end, and if a reform threatened to rock the boat it was usually dropped. Moreover, many of the reforms themselves were simply impractical, for early modern government was very limited in what it could achieve.

Zúñiga and Olivares created a new body, the *Junta* Grande de Reformación,* in August 1622, aiming to eradicate 'vices, abuses and bribes'. Its proposals were embodied in a letter of October 1622, two weeks after Zúñiga's death, and took up many recent (and old) recommendations: sumptuary laws, the abolition of many municipal offices, the closure of brothels, the prohibition of emigration, a national banking scheme (to be financed by a loan of 5 per cent of all wealth), the abolition of both the *millones** and *alcabala* with their replacement by a single consolidated tax, and the provision of soldiers for defence by all the provinces (in embryo, Olivares's Union of Arms). These proposals were not well received. They hurt too many vested interests, had not been discussed by the Cortes*, and were in any event issued by a government that had not only lost goodwill but was positively unpopular. They became law as twenty-three Articles of Reformation in February 1623, but Olivares did agree to call the Cortes to seek their approval. The deputies were disinclined to abolish the *millones* since it was a major source of their power; not surprisingly they opposed the abolition of offices because they were themselves officeholders, and in February 1624 they killed the banking scheme by refusing to fund it. Given the impracticality of closing all brothels and preventing all emigration, and the merchant community's objections to protectionism, no part of the reform package was well received, and as the need for money was paramount Olivares had to retreat on many of the proposals. In 1624, the single tax was abandoned and the government reverted to the *millones*. The failure of this scheme to match income and expenditure by guaranteeing a large and fixed tax yield marked the end of the Count-Duke's attempt to put the crown's finances on a sounder basis. The problem with all reform proposals was that any change to the existing economic and social structure was bound to jeopardize the interests of one group or another.

Olivares returned to the theme of reform in his Great Memorial which he drew up for the King on 25 December 1624. In this the Count-Duke recapitulated many reform proposals that had already failed, but he also revealed what was to be the most abiding theme of his reformism: unity. For Olivares the diversity of the Spanish Monarchy was its real weakness, and a greater concentration of power at the centre was the answer [**doc. 13**]. There had long been a feeling that the other kingdoms were not pulling their weight, and in the most famous passage of the document, the King was exhorted to become King of all Spain and to 'reduce these kingdoms' to the style and laws of Castile' [**doc. 14**]. Were Olivares's proposals the offer of a genuine partnership with reciprocal benefits or simply a blatant attempt at Castilianization? Olivares himself said: 'I am not *nacional,* that is something for children' (quoted in **28**, p. 74), and it has been argued that a partnership was his intention [**doc. 14**]. However, there is little evidence of practical progress in this direction. Olivares made no attempt to break the Castilian monopoly of offices or open up trade with the New World. His proposals showed little sympathy for or understanding of the local identity and loyalties that most people felt in the regions. Indeed, what is striking about Olivares's plans is how unrealistic they were, though admittedly he advocated only a gradual implementation of them. The first step was his proposal for the Union of Arms, a form of collective defence, on 15 October 1625. This document was a practical response to a dire military emergency (**99**). In 1625 Spain found itself at war with both England and France, as well as the Dutch, and accordingly Olivares proposed the creation of a large army of 140,000 men supplied by a quota system from the constituent parts of the Monarchy [**doc. 15**]. These men would not be permanently under arms but would be given training and be called up if any part of the Monarchy was attacked. Olivares showed little finesse in trying to get these proposals accepted; he devised a very tight schedule whereby the King would address the Aragonese, Valencian and Catalan Cortes* in quick succession at the beginning of 1626. The proposals were greeted with the greatest suspicion and Olivares's methods did not endear him to anyone. In March, Valencia was persuaded by the lavish distribution of titles and offices to pay for soldiers, but only for 1,666 men instead of the 6,000 proposed (**58**). The crown accepted this, but subsequently the Cortes decided on a subsidy of 72,000* ducats instead of men. This ran counter to the whole spirit of the Union of Arms, but was nevertheless immediately accepted. The Aragonese eventually adopted a similar solution in the amount of 144,000 ducats. The Catalans, however, would not pay anything.

Despite the setbacks, the King decreed the inauguration of the Union of Arms on 25 July 1626. In the New World as in the Old the Union translated into a new tax; Peru was to raise 350,000 ducats*, Mexico 250,000, to be applied to naval defence (**42**, ch. 10). In Europe, Sardinia and Majorca joined voluntarily in 1626, but Flanders did not accept until the end of 1627. Brussels actually agreed to raise 12,000 men, but this was rather meaningless since Flanders had always provided about that number for its defence (**71**, p. 137). The Union was also applied to Portugal, Burgundy (Franche-Comté) and Spanish Italy (Milan, Naples and Sicily) but its precise application was compromised by the

Mantuan War of 1628–31, when money was needed rather than men.

Clearly, Olivares's plan for the Union of Arms as it was originally envisaged was a failure. But the principle, that all the realms should contribute men and money to the defence of the Monarchy, was strenuously applied, out of necessity as well as policy. It was not an original idea, but the scale and extent of its application came to represent a new departure, and lived on after Olivares, because of the continuing military emergency. Olivares, it has been claimed, 'scored a permanent triumph with his policy of making Valencia bear a little more of the expenses of the Monarchy' (**15**) as he did in the New World (**42**). However, it is in Italy that we witness the most dramatic changes. Between 1630 and 1650 it has been calculated that Naples and Sicily provided an average of 4 million ducats* and 6,000 men every year. By far the lion's share was provided by the Kingdom of Naples – the *Regno*. Between 1631 and 1643 it sent 11 million ducats just to Milan for the Army of Lombardy, and that figure does not include men, arms and supplies. Sicily, though not as wealthy, was contributing a million ducats annually by the end of the 1630s. However, this was a process that had begun in 1620, predating the Union, to counter the shortfall from the Indies, and it escalated more as a response to the military situation than to pressure for reform. Similarly, when the Basque lands and Navarre were mobilized in 1636–38 this was also a response to the military emergency, not the Union of Arms. Olivares was clearly able to tap the resources of the Monarchy on a scale that had not been attempted hitherto and this was the essence of his achievement. Yet Olivares's vision of an integrated Monarchy was seen by many as Castilian exploitation, and herein lay the problem. Rigorous fiscal exploitation led not to greater integration, but to near disintegration.

## Years of success, 1621–25

The end of the Truce with the Dutch in April 1621 did not lead to the immediate outbreak of fighting on land. However, hostilities recommenced in August 1621 and the government was forced to coin *vellón**, sequester private capital and reduce interest rates on *juros** and *censos** in order to finance the forthcoming campaign. Given the fact that the cumulative *juro* debt in 1623 was 112 million ducats* (up 30 per cent since 1598), and that many revenues were pledged to 1625, it is clear that Spain could ill afford to prosecute the war. The financial expedients undertaken in 1621 enabled Spinola to launch the land campaign. He took Jülich in January 1622, but when in the summer he descended upon Bergen-op-Zoom he failed to take it and in the process lost 9,000 men. This has been described as the 'first severe Spanish defeat since the loss of the Armada' (**41**, p. 986). It certainly shook Spinola, who remained largely inactive until he besieged Breda in 1624.

With the death of Zúñiga in October 1622, Olivares came to control foreign policy. Although he had not been responsible for the decisions of 1618 to 1621 there is no doubt that he endorsed them. He was able to defuse the Valtelline* crisis by replacing Spanish with Papal troops (1623), but the complications surrounding the fate of James I's son-in-law, the Elector Palatine, were made worse by the Emperor's decision to transfer Frederick's title to Maximilian of Bavaria. This proved a major obstacle in the way of improving Anglo-Spanish relations, despite the unexpected arrival of the Prince of Wales and the Duke of Buckingham in the Spanish capital in 1623. They had come to seek a marriage alliance, but they left disillusioned and intent on war (**59**).

With the ominous deterioration of Anglo-Spanish relations came the French invasion of the Valtelline* and the Dutch capture of Bahía in Brazil (both in 1624). In addition, the French made alliances with England and the Dutch to add to the agreements with Venice and Savoy. By 1625, it appeared that there was a formidable anti-Habsburg coalition in the making. However, as it turned out, 1625 proved to be something of an *annus mirabilis* for Spain. The Count-Duke resisted calls for a declaration of war on France despite a Franco-Savoyard descent on Genoa in March, though it is likely he aided the Huguenots who rose in revolt against Louis XIII (**29**, p. 227). Genoa was subsequently relieved by a combined land and sea operation, and in May Bahía was recaptured from the Dutch. When Olivares learnt of this success in July he was prompted to remark that 'God is Spanish' (quoted in **29**, p. 227), though the size of the Spanish expedition (fifty-two ships, 12,500 men) – 'the largest force to have crossed to the new world' (**40**, p. 131) – might have had something to do with it. Spinola captured Breda in June after a nine-month siege, and both triumphs were immortalized by the court painter, Velázquez. Further successes followed in the autumn; in October the Dutch failed to capture Puerto Rico and in November a large English expedition of ninety vessels failed to capture Cadiz when the English soldiers discovered large vats of wine and rapidly became incapacitated (**29**). The King in his message to the Council of Castile in 1626 could scarcely conceal his jubilation [**doc. 16**]. Moreover, given Spain's chronic financial situation the supreme effort made in 1625 was 'little short of astonishing' (**52**, p. 216).

The aftermath of 1625 was something of a disappointment. Olivares estimated that to sustain the war effort in 1626 would cost in excess of 14 million ducats\*, and the inability to raise that amount of money, combined with the failure of the Union of Arms, led to a strategic rethinking. The capture of Breda had opened the way to peace negotiations, but in the full flush of victory Olivares threw this opportunity away by raising the Spanish terms. He now demanded not only Dutch withdrawal from the Indies and the reopening of the Scheldt, but some token acknowledgement of Spanish overlordship of the United Provinces and permission for the public practice of Catholicism (**40**). Needless to say the Dutch were not impressed by these terms. Given the parlous financial situation, Olivares decided to scale down the land campaign and step up economic and naval warfare. Dutch vessels were expelled from Spanish territories and an embargo placed on all Dutch goods and assets, and Dunkirk was strengthened as a base for the Flanders armada. This fleet, which eventually numbered twenty-four ships in addition to a large number of privateers, was designed not only to enforce the blockade of the Dutch coast, but also to attack Dutch shipping and disrupt trade. Between 1626 and 1634 it is estimated that 1,835 vessels were captured by the Dunkirkers. Moreover, the embargo seems to have been quite effective as well, and it was conducted with extra vigour after the establishment of the Seville Admiralty Board or *Almirantazgo* in 1624 (**40**). Not content with these successes Olivares envisaged carrying the trade war into that other great area of Dutch commerce, the Baltic. He planned united Spanish-Imperial action to establish a naval base on the north German coastline, in order to wrest from the Dutch their lucrative trade in timber and grain. But Vienna had other interests and Spain, as on other occasions, offered far more than it received. Once again Olivares had demonstrated his capacity for broad vision and the grandiose scheme, but little grasp of what was really possible.

The years of success had been bought at a heavy price, and the triumphs of 1625 in particular had put an enormous strain on Spanish finances. As the government could not finance the war and service the debt, a bankruptcy seemed likely. In fact, Olivares handled the bankruptcy\* of January 1627 with some skill by turning to Portuguese *converso*\* families. Their competition with the Genoese led to an immediate reduction in interest rates and gave the government greater flexibility. The Portuguese came to be responsible for about 60 per cent of loans and, together with the increased contribution of Naples and Sicily, were the key to the continuing viability of the Spanish Monarchy throughout the difficult 1630s (**7**, **99**). These moves were accompanied, in 1628, by a savage deflation which entailed a 50 per-cent reduction in the nominal value of *vellón*\* coinage. Despite Olivares's skill in extricating the crown from financial ruin, however, it is clear that what the Monarchy needed above all was peace.

Richelieu also needed peace, and in 1626 the Treaty of Monzón ended the war in Italy by restoring the *status quo*. This was really a victory for Spain, as France now abandoned its allies, Venice, Savoy and the Dutch. But the scaling-down of the land war in Flanders [**doc. 5**] encouraged the Dutch to go on the offensive and they took Oldenzaal in 1626 and Grol in 1627. In December 1626 Olivares declared that 'peace with honour' was his new objective, yet when the Dutch offered an unconditional ceasefire in 1627 Olivares opposed acceptance on the grounds that it might block the way to a full peace. This was another missed opportunity and it precipitated the return to Madrid of Ambrosio Spinola. The King's illness in 1627 weakened Olivares's position, and it looked for a while as though he might fall. However, the King recovered and, as 1628 approached, the Count-Duke saw cause for optimism. Spanish power and influence were as high as they had ever been, and the Emperor had succeeded in knocking Denmark out of the war. Olivares now hoped for a general peace guaranteed by a league between Spain, the Emperor and the German princes (**29**).

## Years of setbacks, 1628–39

'At the beginning of 1628 the Spanish Monarchy could continue to look upon itself as the greatest political power in the world' (**22**, p. 93), but from this date Spain suffered a number of setbacks. The War of Mantuan Succession (1628–31) ended in failure, and the conjunction of the capture of the silver fleet (1628) with the war in Italy enabled the Dutch to enjoy a period of considerable success (1629–32). Thereafter the Spanish position recovered, and Philip and Olivares could be reasonably satisfied with the years 1633 to 1636 despite the outbreak of war with France in 1635. The year 1637 was a bad one in the Netherlands, but the Monarchy was more than able to hold its own in 1638. However, the continuation and expansion of the war put an enormous strain on the fabric of the entire Monarchy. Olivares made heroic efforts to raise money to sustain the struggle, but his inability to make even a single truce, let alone peace, precipitated a partial collapse in 1640.

At the end of December 1627 Vincenzo II Gonzaga, the Duke of Mantua and Marquis of Montferrat, died with no direct heir and left all his lands to his French (and closest male) relative, the Duke of Nevers. The two states were contiguous to the duchy of Milan and were therefore of some strategic significance for Spain's communications and its domination of the Italian peninsula. Although Nevers was a Frenchman it would hardly have been in his interest to adopt an anti-Spanish position. What is surprising is that Olivares, that inveterate planner, had made no plans for Nevers's succession even though the Duke of Mantua's death had been anticipated for some time. It would appear that he allowed himself to be drawn into conflict by Gonzalo Fernández de Córdoba, the governor of Milan, who had made a deal with Savoy for the partition of Montferrat. Olivares seems to have believed that Don Gonzalo was already on the march (**28**) and that a cheap victory, gained at a time when Louis XIII was bogged down besieging La Rochelle, would be good for Spain's *reputación**. But Gonzalo de Córdoba was not on the march, and when he finally got round to besieging the Fortress of Casale in Montferrat in mid-May 1628 the defenders were well prepared and the siege eventually failed. The intervention in Mantua coincided with the arrival in Madrid of Ambrosio Spinola, the commander of the Army of Flanders, in February 1628. With his immense experience and sense of realism Spinola was able to dominate the Council of State and influence the impressionable Philip IV. He argued against involvement in Mantua and in favour of peace with the Dutch. The latter position the King now adopted in defiance of Olivares. It seems that the Dutch were prepared to acknowledge some relationship with Spain in return for a twelve- or twenty-year truce (**40**), but Olivares insisted on his unrealistic terms of 1625, partly out of fear of surrendering the policy initiative to Spinola. Spinola riposted by refusing to return to Brussels without either serious peace negotiations or substantial reinforcements. At this point the initiative slipped from Spain's grasp, for in September 1628 the Dutchman Piet Heyn captured the silver fleet in Matanzas Bay off Cuba [**doc. 17**]. This catastrophe prompted Philip IV to comment, 'whenever I speak of the disaster the blood runs cold in my veins, not for the

loss of treasure, but because we lost our *reputación** in that in-
famous defeat' (quoted in **52**, p. 208). Moreover, it provided the
Dutch with an enormous windfall and encouraged them to forget
about peace negotiations and launch an offensive. Belatedly
Olivares agreed to the principle of an armistice and gave the
Archduchess Isabella full powers to negotiate. But it was too late.
In February 1629 France invaded Savoy, and in March Charles
Emmanuel, the Duke, capitulated. A month later Gonzalo de
Córdoba lifted the siege of Casale. Later that year the Stadholder,
Frederick Henry, whose forces now outnumbered the Army of
Flanders by two to one, launched an offensive. Wesel fell to the
Dutch in August and Bois-le-Duc ('s Hertogenbosch) in
September. By this stage, given the absence of Spinola – who had
left to take up the command in Italy in July – Spanish authority in
Flanders was on the verge of collapse.

What is remarkable about this period of setbacks is that Olivares
emerged from them with more power than ever before. He was
able to do this by disclaiming responsibility for the Mantuan War
(**98**) and blaming all the setbacks on Spinola [**doc. 18**]. Moreover,
the coincidence of setbacks with Philip IV's greater involvement in
decision-making may have seriously undermined the King's
already fragile confidence. The reverses continued. The province
of Pernambuco in Brazil was captured by the Dutch in 1630, a
severe blow to the Portuguese, to whom it had formerly belonged.
The French invaded Savoy again and took the fortress of Pinerolo
in March 1630. Spinola laid siege to Casale but died in September
as plague ravaged the area. Olivares now accepted the inevitable
and came to terms with France at the Treaty of Cherasco in June
1631. Nevers was recognized as the Duke of Mantua and France
held on to Pinerolo, thereby gaining a foothold in Italy. For Spain
the war had been a disaster. Not only had it cost 10 million ducats*
and gained the Monarchy nothing; it had also sabotaged the possibility of an honourable peace with the Dutch by diverting
resources at a crucial moment (**29**), and it had led to the strengthening of Richelieu's position in France.

The end of the Mantuan War (and peace with England in 1630)
did not mean an end to Olivares's troubles, for in 1632 Frederick
Henry captured Venlo and Roermond, then Maastricht and
Limburg. The Archduchess Isabella, nominal ruler of the
Netherlands, succumbed to enormous pressure and convened the
States-General in Brussels in September 1632. This body took it
upon itself to open peace negotiations with the United Provinces,

**The Netherlands, 1621–1648**

0    50    100    150 km

EAST FRIESLAND
Emden

GRONINGEN

FRIESLAND    TERRITORY OF DRENTE

Ems

Lingen

HOLLAND

Enkhuizen
Hoorn

OVERIJSSEL

IJssel    Oldenzaal

Amsterdam    Deventer

Haarlem

Leiden    UTRECHT    GELDERLAND    Grol

The Hague    Utrecht    Arnhem
Delft    Rhine    Schenkenschans

Rotterdam    Waal    Nijmegen    Cleves    Rees
Wesel
ZEALAND    Dordrecht    MEIERIJ    Gennep    Rheinberg
's Hertogenbosch    Orsoy
Breda    Eindhoven    Geldern
Middelburg    Bergen-op-Zoom    Venlo    Düsseldorf
Flushing    Zandvliet    Roermond
Brugge    Hulst    Antwerp    Maastricht
Ostend    Sas van Gent    Julich
Dunkirk    Ghent    BRABANT    LIMBURG
FLANDERS    Lys    Louvain    LIÈGE
WALLOON    Scheldt    Brussels
FLANDERS    TOURNAI    Liège
Lille    HAINAULT    NAMUR
ARTOIS    CAMBRAI
Arras    Sambre    LUXEMBURG

Meuse

| | |
|---|---|
| Spanish Netherlands | |
| Independent Bishopric of Liège | |
| Territories conquered or reconquered by the Dutch 1626–48 | |

but fortunately for Olivares the Dutch came up with a totally unreasonable package of demands, including complete Spanish withdrawal from the entire Netherlands. Olivares now determined to send a powerful army to restore royal authority and enable him to bargain with the Dutch from strength (**40**).

Spanish setbacks during these years were not only caused by the extent of the Monarchy's commitments, which meant that resources were spread too thin, but also by a lack of money. In a bout of intensive fiscalism in 1631–32, Olivares increased revenue by extending the tax burden to the nobles and clergy and putting pressure on them to contribute soldiers to royal service. In 1631 lesser nobles were allowed to commute their military obligations into cash payments (the *lanzas* tax), and in May of the same year a new impost, the *media anata**, a fee on new offices, was introduced. Also in 1631 the *millones** was abolished (again) and a salt tax introduced. This was not a success, however, and led to serious riots in Vizcaya in 1631. Accordingly, in 1632 Olivares summoned the Cortes*. On this occasion he demanded that the delegates come with full powers to vote, and they were then browbeaten into restoring the *millones* at 4 million ducats* per annum for six years. Olivares also ordered another *donativo** – the third of the reign – and another sequestration of private silver in Seville. Whatever their impact on Castile's economy, in the short term these measures all helped to reinforce royal credit and expand royal income at a time when the international situation was grave. The British ambassador Hopton, writing in 1634, estimated that the crown's revenues had doubled in the previous four years (**29**, p. 453). This remarkable achievement by Olivares restored the military initiative to the Spanish Monarchy.

Following the death of the Archduchess Isabella, in Brussels in December 1633, it was decided to appoint Philip IV's brother, the Cardinal Infante Ferdinand, as governor. In April 1634 the Cortes* voted 4 million ducats* for the campaign, and in July the King's brother set out from Milan (**29**). In September he linked up with the new imperial commander, Archduke Ferdinand, at Nördlingen where their joint armies of 33,000 inflicted a decisive defeat on the 25,000 Swedes. This 'greatest victory of our time', as Olivares put it, cleared the Swedes out of southern Germany and enabled the Cardinal Infante to reach Brussels, which he entered in triumph in November (**75**, pp. 140–1). Spanish prestige was now high, once again, and it would have been well if Olivares had seized the opportunity to negotiate peace with the Dutch on favourable terms. Instead he proposed going on the offensive. Even worse, he pushed France into open war.

Richelieu had stated in 1629: 'our constant aim must be to check the advance of Spain... this must be done in the long term, very discreetly' (quoted in **54**, p.84). France was surrounded by Spanish territory – the Netherlands in the north, Franche-Comté in the east, Spain itself in the south – and the communications between them which were a lifeline to Spain were a noose to France (**28**). Yet Richelieu also described direct confrontation as the 'worst possible situation that could arise' (quoted in **79**, p. 95). War by proxy served French interest best, and by funding the Dutch and the Swedes Richelieu deflected Habsburg attention and enabled France to undertake territorial annexation in Alsace and Lorraine. By 1634 Olivares had become increasingly exasperated by Richelieu's anti-Spanish moves (**98**). He could not understand how a cardinal, of all people, could conspire with heretics to wreck his vision of a Christendom at peace under the protection of the King of Spain. When Olivares drew up his financial dispositions for 1635 he made provision for war with France but it is clear from the figures (1.7 million ducats* out of 8.4 million) that only a diversionary campaign was envisaged. However, tension continued to rise. In February 1635 Richelieu made a formal alliance with the Dutch. The following month, Spanish troops carried off the Elector of Trier, who was under French protection. Richelieu, believing that the Spanish were about to declare war, decided to get in first and using the Trier incident he made a formal declaration on 19 May. He expected Olivares to request negotiations, but Olivares, buoyed up by the victory at Nördlingen, was prepared for war. He felt that the experienced Habsburg armies would win a quick victory; the overthrow of Richelieu was all that was required (**79, 98**).

Olivares needed to bring about Richelieu's fall very quickly since Spain could not afford a war of attrition, and in any event the main priority remained the Netherlands. France had a larger population than the entire Spanish Monarchy in Europe (20 million against 15 million), internal lines of communication and greater taxable wealth. Indeed, in 1635 alone, the first year of the war, France spent over 41 million *livres tournais* (**4**) (possibly 13–14 million ducats – see note on coinage) on war expenditure. When we compare this figure with Olivares's dispositions for 1635 of 8.4 million ducats, reduced to 7.25 million by November 1635 (**29**), we can appreciate the potential disparity between the two sides.

Admittedly Spanish resources were augmented by moneys raised in the various territories; however, it still seems that France could raise more money for the war than the government in Madrid. Moreover, with the Grace of Alais in 1629, Richelieu had finally brought the Wars of Religion to an end, and France was more stable than it had been at any time during the history of the Spanish Monarchy. Despite this, the war began badly for France and both campaigns in Flanders and Italy ended disastrously.

Despite suffering from insomnia and depression, Olivares threw himself into the task of raising more money for this war and subjected Castile to another bout of 'intensive fiscalism' in 1635–36. A fourth *donativo*\* brought some response, and he also fell back on the usual expedients of sale of offices and titles, withholding interest on *juros*\*, tampering with the currency, and requisitions. The restamping of sixteenth-century *vellón*\* coinage brought the government a profit of 4 million ducats\* in 1636, but coming at a time of poor harvests it had a disastrous impact on the economy. So too did Olivares's interference in the transatlantic trade. This had continued to decline in volume and value during the 1630s, and silver remittances to the treasury were irregular and failed to live up to expectations [**doc. 8**]. Between 1635 and 1637 the Count-Duke requisitioned 2 million ducats of private silver (in exchange for *vellón* coinage) and on top of this also imposed forced loans in 1636 and 1637. In addition, he came up with a new tax, the paper tax, to be applied from 1637. Ignoring the long-term economic damage this was doing, it is clear that these measures had the required effect in the short term, for Spanish forces now exceeded 150,000 (see **29**, p. 509).

In order to relieve French pressure on Franche-Comté, which had come under assault from Condé, the Cardinal Infante decided to launch a diversionary attack on France. But 'what had originally been intended as no more than a preventive strike suddenly assumed major significance as French resistance crumbled' (**29**, p. 521). By August the Cardinal Infante had captured Corbie, 80 miles from Paris, Condé withdrew from Franche-Comté and Imperial forces moved into French Burgundy in September. However, the French recovered, the Imperial forces were recalled to face the Swedes, Corbie was retaken in November, and the Cardinal Infante withdrew from France. In 1637 Richelieu offered a truce based on the *status quo*, but Olivares had high expectations for the forthcoming season and still hoped for a favourable peace settlement. Once again the Count-Duke's optimism proved to be

51

misplaced, for although the Spaniards had some success in Italy, an attempt to invade France from Catalonia ended in defeat at Leucate (September 1637). Most devastating of all, Breda, that symbol of Spain's *annus mirabilis*, fell to Frederick Henry in October.

However, the Monarchy recovered in 1638, inflicting defeats on both French and Dutch forces. The year 1639 also opened well, but an attempt to secure the 'English Road' (**103**) – that is, the sea route from Spain to Flanders [**doc. 6**] – ended in disaster. A Spanish armada of about 100 ships set sail on 6 September and ten days later engaged Tromp's Dutch fleet in the Channel. After a three-day battle the Spanish were forced into the Downs where many of the ships were destroyed by Tromp, while others were lost or damaged in a storm. As if this was not bad enough, news reached Spain of failure in Brazil, where the Count of La Torre with eighty-six ships and 10,000 men not only failed to retake Pernambuco but in January 1640 allowed himself to be bested by a Dutch fleet of half the size. These disasters were blamed on Olivares, who found himself under increasing criticism.

Despite the huge cost of the war, the Spanish state was still able to mobilize funds on a massive scale. In 1638 the Cortes* was informed that the crown's expenditure over the previous six years had been 72 million ducats* (12 million per annum) of which 21 million had gone to Flanders (3.5 million per annum). In the face of invasion the delegates were browbeaten into voting a renewal of the *millones** for six years at 4 million ducats per annum. As we have seen, the Monarchy was able to put together two large armadas in 1639. In addition, the Army of Milan probably numbered about 40,000 and by January 1640 the Army of Flanders reached nearly 90,000 men [**doc. 5**] – the largest force assembled there since the beginning of the troubles in the 1570s. These achievements are 'a remarkable testimonial both to the Count-Duke's determination, and to the continuing capacity of an apparently exhausted Spanish Monarchy to raise or mobilize funds' (**29**, p. 517). But France and Spain were now locked into a war of attrition, and the question was, who would break first?

## A year of disasters, 1640

The fiscal strains on Spain were by now enormous [**doc. 19**]. The Indies trade collapsed in the aftermath of the Spanish naval defeats and complaints were coming in from all over the

Monarchy, suggesting that taxation had reached saturation point. The paper tax had to be withdrawn soon after its introduction in Sicily in 1639, and in Naples the budgetary process had begun to break down (**14**), prompting the viceroy, the Duke of Medina de las Torres, to warn that the nobility might at some stage in the future put *patria* before *rex* (**29**). However, Olivares was uncomprehending and disdainful of this attitude, and his reaction was to press ahead with integration. This had disastrous consequences in Catalonia.

Catalonia had always been a fiscal problem, but the Catalans' resistance to the Union of Arms in 1626 and again in 1632 made them a political problem as well. In addition, after 1635 they became a strategic problem, as they were now in the front line against France (**61**). Olivares was not discouraged; he believed that under pressure of war the Catalans would be forced to participate and thereby demonstrate their loyalty. In 1639, therefore, he deliberately chose Catalonia as the principal war front: the Union of Arms would be forced upon its inhabitants. An army had been raised in Castile to defend the Catalan frontier, and the people of the principality were forced to pay for it in kind – with food, billets and contributions. At Olivares's insistence another force was raised from within Catalonia, but the Catalans refused to send it supplies, or to provide replacements for the missing and the dead. Instead, they appealed to their *fueros** or 'constitutions' which they claimed were being infringed. Olivares became increasingly exasperated: 'By now I am nearly at my wits end, but I say, and I shall be saying on my deathbed, that if the constitutions do not allow this, then the devil take the constitutions' (October 1639, quoted in **23**, p. 375). This flouting of local laws and privileges at a time when severe drought threatened the harvest was 'foolishly provocative' (**74**, p. 259). In January the Catalan *Audiencia** had declared that billeting was illegal, but Olivares was scathing in his response [**doc. 20**]. Throughout the early part of 1640 there were clashes between troops and civilians in many parts of the principality, and in April a royal official was burnt to death at a village in the province of Gerona. The *tercios** retaliated on 14 May by destroying the whole village, but their action roused the entire countryside to arms. A peasant army, constantly growing in size, forced the soldiers to retreat, and moved on to occupy Barcelona. 'A wave of social revolution swept over the principality' (**52**, p. 238), and on 7 June Santa Coloma, the viceroy himself, was murdered as he attempted to flee Barcelona. This was not so much a rebellion as chaos, and as the slide into anarchy continued the upper echelons of Catalan society sought to recover the reins of control. Olivares decided to use force to crush the revolt in Catalonia, and the Catalans thereupon appealed for help to the French. In January 1641 they formally swore allegiance to Louis XIII as Count of Barcelona, and in the same month they repulsed the Castilian army at the battle of Montjuich outside Barcelona. For the next decade Catalonia remained divorced from Spain.

The Catalans eventually returned to their allegiance, in 1652. Not so, however, the Portuguese. In Portugal, as in Catalonia, it was the application of the Union of Arms that started the rot (**88, 97**). Prior to this, the union had not suffered any serious strain at all. However, in 1628 a new subsidy of 200,000 *cruzados* per annum (approximately 160,000 ducats*) was imposed over six years, and this, together with the threat of a salt tax, led to violent protests in 1628–30. Olivares taxed the Church from 1633 and imposed a new tax, the *media anata**, on officeholders; soon nobles were being browbeaten for direct contributions to the war effort. In 1634 a new administration containing many Castilian advisers took over under the nominal leadership of Margaret of Savoy, Philip IV's cousin, with the task of introducing a new range of sales taxes to achieve an overall annual revenue of 500,000 *cruzados* (400,000 ducats). Madrid's increased demands were coming at a time of reduced prosperity. The loss of Pernambuco in 1630 led to the Dutch appropriating almost half the lucrative sugar trade, and the failure to recover this territory in 1640 (albeit by a Portuguese-led expedition) clearly undermined the allegiance to Philip IV (Philip III in Portugal). The example of the Catalans must also have had an impact on Portuguese aspirations, but the Portuguese had what the Catalans lacked – namely, a unity created by devotion to the old ruling house. The nearest in line was John, Duke of Braganza, who declared himself King John IV of Portugal in December 1640. When he heard the news the Count-Duke displayed his usual disbelief, once again demonstrating his remoteness from reality. He had described the Portuguese as 'essentially faithful', but they were in fact essentially Portuguese. Here was a second Netherlands, but much closer to home.

These twin blows of Catalonia and Portugal marked an end to Spanish hegemony in Europe. The revolts seemed to presage the disintegration of the Monarchy; indeed, the British ambassador reported, 'the greatness of this Monarchy is near to an end' (quoted in **30**, p. 131) [**doc. 21**]. Not for the first time, however, reports of Spain's demise proved to be exaggerated, and the Monarchy eventually recovered, though Spain never again enjoyed its earlier *reputación** as the foremost power in the western world. But the collapse, though not total, was real enough, and Olivares's attempt to impose his vision of 'Union' by riding roughshod over local rights and privileges at a time of great stress and economic hardship undoubtedly bears the major responsibility for it. This makes it all the more astonishing that the Count-Duke was not immediately dismissed. The fact that he survived underlines the extent of Philip IV's dependency on him.

## The fall of Olivares

The rebellions in Catalonia and Portugal seemed to herald the collapse of the Monarchy. However, the remaining constituent parts, although under enormous strain, stayed loyal and the war continued. The Armies of Flanders and Milan remained formidable forces and Spain's enemies made remarkably little progress. The Dutch signed a ten-year truce with the Portuguese which effectively destroyed the Spanish embargo as Portuguese ports were thrown open to Dutch shipping, and the latter soon recovered control of the salt trade. However, the aftermath of the Spanish naval disasters of 1639–40 saw a remarkable revival and re-expansion of the Flemish armada and privateers, and the level of Dutch losses rose appreciably in the early 1640s [**doc. 22**]. On land the Dutch took Gennep in 1641, but after this they remained on the defensive. The French army had finally enjoyed some success, taking Arras and most of Artois in 1640, and Perpignan, the capital of Roussillon, in 1642. However, in the same year Don Francisco de Melo, the new governor of Flanders (the Cardinal Infante died in 1641), inflicted a significant defeat on the French at Honnecourt. 'The 1642 campaign contributed to the gradual recovery of Spanish prestige in Europe' (**40**, p. 316).

This recovery came too late to save Olivares. By the autumn of 1641 the effect of cumulative failure was beginning to tell on his mental health, and Hopton, the British ambassador, reported that 'he is so overlaid with care ... that his judgment begins to break' (quoted **29**, p. 622) [**doc. 23**]. However, the Count-Duke managed to keep the ship of state afloat with more loans, and his Portuguese bankers remitted 12 million ducats* to the crown in the years 1641–42 (**7**). Their future was dependent upon his, and Olivares's ability to raise funds made him seemingly indispensable. But in

January 1642 it was reported that the King was working on his papers alone, and this unusual display of independence inspired members of the *Junta Grande* to encourage him to leave for the front. Finally in April (after expressing a desire to go since 1629!) the King departed. 'Philip's decision was hailed as the first independent action he had taken in his life' (**29**, p. 628), and much of his experience in the months ahead convinced him that he could function without the Count-Duke. Olivares had, of course, already lost the support of everyone else, especially the grandees. In the late 1630s his heavy taxation had brought about a steady exodus of the nobility from the court, culminating in the 'strike of the grandees' (*huelga de grandes*) in 1640. On Christmas Day 1642 only a single grandee took his place in the royal chapel. The King must have got the message, even if Olivares did not. On 16 January 1643, Olivares's secretary Carnero wrote: 'My master is utterly exhausted and shattered, although, even with the water over him, he still keeps swimming' (quoted in **28**, p. 154). The following day the King gave him leave to retire. The Count-Duke was banished to the country and he died, fat and insane, at Toro in 1645.

There is no doubt that Olivares was a failure, and he failed on a monumental scale. The very thing he sought to prevent, the collapse of Spanish hegemony, he actually brought about. His reforms were largely unrealistic and in any event were not compatible with the belligerent foreign policy he was conducting; and his foreign policy was a failure because he was unable to compromise and make peace. Peace, as Lerma knew, was what Spain needed most.

> Temperamentally the Count-Duke seems to have found it hard to take clear, sharp decisions, without accompanying them with qualifying formulas and subsidiary proposals which either weakened or subverted the line of action he proposed to take. This happened time and time again with the Dutch. Hoping to get a better deal, he would throw away such chances as existed of securing any deal at all. (**29**, p. 587).

Olivares's concern for *reputación*\* not only prevented him from making peace; it also involved Spain in endless wars it could not afford. He was not a clear thinker – his *consultas*\* are rambling and convoluted – and he was subject to wild swings of mood. His optimism gave him unrealistic expectations; his melancholia came along with disappointment when these expectations were not realized.

What, then, can be said in Olivares's favour? There is no doubt that the one reform he remained true to, the Union of Arms, had a measure of success. He did get the other territories to contribute more to their own defence and the general war effort, particularly Naples and Sicily and the New World. Admittedly this policy eventually led to rebellion and even secession, but it enabled the Monarchy to keep going right through the 1630s and after. Olivares showed great flair as a finance minister; he crushed the Cortes*, taxed the nobles and clergy, and introduced Portuguese bankers into the loan process. He tapped the resources of the Monarchy and kept it going *in extremis*. At a time when ducats meant more than bullets, his ability to raise money made him almost indispensable.

Olivares believed that Spain was in decline and that his duty was to arrest this process. Historians have concluded that he accelerated it. However, we must not make a drama out of a crisis. Olivares pushed the Spanish Monarchy too far, but it was still largely intact and capable of recovery. The loss of hegemony in 1640 did not automatically lead to that of France, for France was in a bad way too. Spain could and did recover, even if things had to get worse initially. The struggle for European hegemony was still undecided.

# 5    The Reign of Philip IV, (2) 1643–65

## Survival, 1643–48

The dismissal of Olivares in 1643 did not lead to any dramatic changes in Spanish policy or Spain's position. The aims remained the same – *conservación** of dynastic rights, the preservation of *reputación** and the search for a just peace (*paz honesta*) (**99**). Philip IV now resolved to rule as well as reign: 'such a good minister must be replaced only by me myself' (quoted in **52**, p. 204). Furthermore, he stated, 'it is better to treat all [ministers] equally, listening to all without favouring one at another's expense.... I am resolved to change the previous mode of government, and although there is no lack of people who wish to become *valido** – a natural ambition amongst men – they are all deceived' (quoted in **99**, pp. 249–50). In practice, however, power came to reside with Olivares's nephew, Don Luis de Haro. He was a softer man than Olivares, relaxed and affable, 'a different *valido*' (**21**). The aristocracy recovered some ground, their fiscal burdens were relaxed but they did not participate in government. Many *juntas** were dissolved and conciliar government revived. Haro was in fact referred to by the King as *primer ministro* in the 1650s, and this term is perhaps to be preferred to *valido* since he did not have the control of patronage or the monopoly of the King's attention that Lerma (with Philip III) and Olivares had had (**99**). However, by 1647 he had clearly established his primacy [**doc. 24**] and could convene the *Junta de Estado* in his house.

The King himself continued to work hard at his papers, and in the period 1643 to 1647 he regularly chaired the *Junta de Estado*. However, it was unusual for him 'to reject or ignore majority advice... on important issues' (**99**, p. 281), and he soon came not only to accept advice, but decisions too (**63, 109, 110**). Philip did in fact intervene more decisively than in the time of Olivares, but unfortunately his interventions – such as his rejection of Haro's novel financial suggestion in 1647, his cowardly execution of the Marquis of Ayamonte (also 1647), his obstinate refusal to make peace with France in 1656, and his obsessive refusal to accept Portuguese independence – were none too impressive. Moreover, after 1661 when he undoubtedly was in control, Spanish fortunes went rapidly downhill.

In the aftermath of Olivares's demise Philip IV clearly became more popular. His regular sojourn at the front improved his image and his stoic fortitude when confronted with the loss of first his wife Queen Isabella in 1644 and then his son Baltasar Carlos in 1646 won the admiration of many. Moreover, in 1647, when he remained in Madrid and helped quarantine the capital from the approaching plague by improving and generating food distribution, his popularity was further enhanced (**99**). His marriage to his niece Queen Mariana of Austria in 1649 was the cause of much celebration. However, this popularity did not persist. With the continuation of the war there was no relief of hardship and resentment at his failure to make peace grew.

Peace was the fervent desire of a mystical Franciscan nun, Sister María de Ágreda, with whom the King conducted a regular correspondence (600 letters) until her death just before his. At least one historian has commented on the irony that 'the head of the world's most powerful state should be swayed by the relatively uninformed opinions of a provincial recluse' (**52**, p. 204), but in fact the influence of Sister María was limited – except perhaps for her denunciation of *validos**. The correspondence was more of a release for the King, a way for him to recite 'his troubles in endless letters of lamentation' (**95**, p. 123) [**doc.25**]. Most of Sister María's advice – for example, to make peace with France and go on a crusade – was ignored.

In 1643, however, peace with France did seem a possibility, for the death of Richelieu in December 1642 was followed six months later by that of his master Louis XIII. As the new ruler, Louis XIV, was only 4 years old a regency government had to be formed, and it was unusual for a regency to continue prosecuting a war. However, the regent, Anne of Austria (who was Philip IV's sister), had come under the influence of Cardinal Mazarin who was Richelieu's replacement. Mazarin, an Italian by birth, dared not risk being blamed for a hasty peace, and opted for a vigorous prosecution of the war (**68**). Between 1643 and 1647 French military expenditure increased dramatically, by some 30 per cent over the previous five years, and in 1643 alone it totalled 48 million *livres* (that is, 12–16 million ducats*, twice Spanish military expenditure). Mazarin was gambling on rapid success, but he underestimated Spanish resilience and overestimated French resources.

In 1643 the governor of Flanders, encouraged by Dutch cutbacks, decided to invade France, but his army was cut to pieces at Rocroi by a larger French force with the loss of nearly 12,000 men [**doc. 26**]. This defeat used to be regarded as the end of Spanish power, but 'for two decades more Spain continued to fight... on a broader range of fronts than any other nation was capable of' (**52**, p. 209). Nevertheless, it put the Army of Flanders on the defensive and in 1644 priority was given to the peninsular campaign – indeed, troops were ferried from Flanders to Castile. In Catalonia Monzón had been recaptured in 1643 and this was followed by Lérida in 1644 where Philip, in a shrewd move, took a solemn oath to observe Catalan rights and privileges. Subsequent French assaults were all repulsed. However, things went from bad to worse in Flanders. In 1645 the French took ten towns, more than the Dutch had taken in two decades, prompting Philip IV to declare, 'peace is necessary, whatever the cost, whatever the price' (quoted in **52**, p. 209). In 1646 Condé went on to take Dunkirk, and now even the Dutch were becoming alarmed at French success.

However, if things were bad for Spain in 1646, they got even worse in 1647–48 with bankruptcy, revolts in Sicily, Naples and Granada, conspiracy in Aragon and widespread plague and death in Andalucía. Given the continuation of the Portuguese and Catalan revolts, it is clear that 1647 was far more serious than 1640; it looked as though the Monarchy really was disintegrating. That it in fact survived says a great deal about its inherent strength.

Spain could not match French expenditure, and by 1644 the revenues had been anticipated as far ahead as 1648. In 1646 Philip felt obliged to summon the Cortes*, but the crown was unable to get its way and the Cortes was dissolved (**99**). Lacking any extension and expansion of the *millones**, and facing a serious slump in the silver return from the Indies, which crippled credit, it was clear by the autumn of 1646 that there was going to be a shortfall of about 5 million ducats* on the following year's projected expenditure. New taxes at a time of harvest catastrophe were ruled out by Haro, who devised a radical scheme to confiscate a quarter of all *juro** equity. The King, however, rejected this idea and opted for bankruptcy* (that is, debt conversion) on 1 October 1647. The principal Genoese bankers were exempted and the real victims were the Portuguese *conversos**. Their downfall was popular in Madrid, but it was shabby treatment after twenty years of helping to keep the Monarchy afloat. The bankruptcy involved the repudiation of 10 million ducats* worth of short-term loans and enabled the Monarchy to weather its severest storm.

The revolt in Sicily was initiated by an outbreak of violence in Palermo in May 1647, caused by bad harvests, high taxes and resentment of noble privilege. The rising was not politically disloyal ('Long live the King and down with taxes and bad government' was the usual cry). Messina, the second largest city, remained loyal (55), the propertied classes rallied to the viceroy, and authority was restored prior to the arrival of Philip's illegitimate son, Don Juan José. Indeed, Sicily's collaboration was important in suppressing the more serious revolt in Naples.

Naples had been subjected to an enormous increase in taxation since the 1620s and the Duke of Medina de las Torres, viceroy in 1637–44, had already warned that fiscal exploitation had reached saturation point. Poor harvests, rising prices, the example of Sicily and a new tax on fruit proved to be the catalyst as towns and peasants rose up in July 1647 against domination and exploitation by the nobility (but not at first against Spanish rule). The viceroy, the Duke of Arcos, fled, leaving control to the nobles, who proclaimed a republic in October but subsequently offered their allegiance to France. In November an unofficial French pretender, the Duke of Guise, arrived and in December a French fleet appeared off the coast. However, after a hard-fought battle the French had to withdraw, and Spanish forces under Don Juan José blockaded the city of Naples. The townspeople began to realize they had little in common with the peasantry, and all who possessed property were increasingly wary of social upheaval. By April 1648 the revolt had collapsed, and although Mazarin had prepared a second, larger expedition which arrived off the coast in August, this proved a fiasco as Neapolitans combined with Spaniards to drive the French off (19, 91, 114). These were remarkable victories for Spain at a difficult time, but they were bought at a price. The new viceroy, the Count of Oñate (son of the famous diplomat, who died in 1645), was unable to exploit the kingdom as his predecessors had done, and Spanish finances were thereby weakened.

In accordance with the decision taken in 1644 to give the Catalan front priority, the size of the Army of Flanders was reduced. By 1647 it was two-thirds what it had been in 1640 [**doc. 5**], and remittances were halved to about 2 million ducats*

(**71**, p. 295). Indeed, the new governor, Archduke Leopold William (1647–55), felt he might not be able to cope were there to be an uprising, and therefore urged peace. The Dutch also wanted peace, for they were increasingly alarmed at the implications of French victories. The Spaniards played on this fear by leaking French proposals to exchange Spanish Flanders for Catalonia. Moreover, the Dutch had made little headway in the East and West Indies in the 1640s, and the Dunkirkers had continued to take a heavy toll of their shipping. From Madrid's point of view the Portuguese revolt had removed Brazil as an obstacle to negotiation, and during 1646 the Spaniards conceded Dutch sovereignty, agreed to Dutch control of the Scheldt and consented to recognize Dutch conquests from Portugal. They would not, however, admit the Dutch to the trade of Spanish America, and they insisted on the right of Catholic worship for the inhabitants of the Meierij (see Map 2). A provisional agreement was signed in January 1647 which was ratified, despite Mazarin's attempts at sabotage, in January 1648. The Treaty of Münster was then formally signed in October (**40, 75**). What had been *de facto* for so long now became *de jure*.

It is often assumed that Mazarin 'excluded' Spain from the Peace of Westphalia. The truth is that Spain had no intention of making peace with France until Catalonia had been regained. So far from signalling the 'ascendancy of France', Westphalia was signed at a time when France was sliding into bankruptcy* and civil war. Spain saw this as an opportunity for recovery.

## Revival, 1649–56

Out of Westphalia there arose a balance of power between France and the Habsburgs (**85**, p. 381), despite the fact that a Spanish offensive on the Flanders front had come to grief at Lens in August. Leopold William lost 9,000 men in this defeat at the hands of Condé; however, the victory for France was more spectacular than decisive, as with the outbreak of civil war in France – the Frondes – there was no possibility of a follow-up. Nevertheless, Spain was forced to scale down its operations in Flanders and a stalemate ensued. In both 1649 and 1650 Mazarin offered Philip peace, but the King insisted on a return to the *status quo ante bellum* (namely, the position in 1635) and would not countenance any concessions. Rather than indulging in Olivares-like obstinacy, it would appear that Philip felt the opportunities for recovery were there for the taking, and he was right. In Italy the French were driven from the *presidios** (1650), and two years later Spanish forces captured the fortress of Casale that had been Olivares's objective in the Mantuan War. In Flanders, Gravelines was taken in May 1652 and in September the Spanish re-took Dunkirk. In 1653 Ypres and Mardyk were recaptured and in 1654, Rocroi, that supposed graveyard of Spanish military might, fell to the Army of Flanders. However, the real prize of these years was the reconquest of Catalonia.

Catalonia had been formally annexed by France and a Bourbon viceroy had been installed in Barcelona. However, the substitution of Louis XIII and later Louis XIV for Philip IV had solved none of Catalonia's problems; the Catalans had merely traded one master for another, harsher one. This was the background to the Spanish campaign which led to the recapture of Barcelona in October 1652. Spain had learnt its lesson and Catalonia was treated gently. Its rights were confirmed, but the province now willingly paid a contribution to the war effort, and Barcelona alone contributed 150,000 ducats* per annum. Twelve years of French occupation had made the Catalans the most anti-French of Spain's provinces.

The year 1652 was something of an *annus mirabilis* for Spain, and the European balance of power seemed to be shifting back in its favour. However, Spanish success had been bought at enormous cost. Philip IV reported to the Cortes* in 1655 that military expenditure between 1649 and 1654 had been 66.8 million ducats* in silver. Indeed, despite the bankruptcy of 1647 the treasury was in trouble again by 1650. Inflation was rampant, and 98 per cent of the coinage was copper, for Spain, the owner of the American silver mines, had no silver. The crown seized 1 million ducats of private bullion imports from the Indies and anticipated revenue to 1655. It also expanded *vellón** output, to pay for the campaign in Catalonia, but then in 1652 instituted another savage deflation. Monetary disorder could hardly have been worse. Then the government announced yet another bankruptcy* only five years after the previous one.

Financial failure explains why the Spanish Monarchy was unable to follow up its successes of 1652. Indeed, the conjunction of Spanish bankruptcy* with French recovery from the Frondes ensured that a balance of power would be restored. However, whether or not 'power' is the correct word is debatable; in these years France and Spain came to resemble two exhausted boxers clinging to each other, hanging on to the ropes, trading the occasional punch, but ultimately waiting for the bell. Spain could not go on the offensive, but it could defend itself, while France, after the Frondes, was unable to pursue Mazarin's grand objectives. In 1656, therefore, Mazarin decided to send Hugues de Lionne to Madrid to open negotiations.

## The Treaty of the Pyrenees, 1659

Lionne's mission to Madrid in 1656 was the most serious attempt to break the deadlock thus far. Talks lasted for three months and came close to an agreement. However, against the advice of his ministers Philip IV rejected a settlement (**63**, p. 169), for he refused to abandon Condé, who had deserted to Spain in 1652 and was now commander of the Army of Flanders. This was unfortunate, since after 1656 the balance of power tipped back in the direction of France.

One reason for this was the impact of plague on Naples, which had come to play a significant part in the war effort of the Spanish Monarchy (second only to Castile), regularly providing 3.5 million ducats* per annum. The city of Naples itself was one of the largest in the world, second only to Paris in Europe, with a population approaching 400,000. But it was also the most crowded, and when the plague struck it did so with devastating effect. At its peak, in the summer of 1656, 10–15,000 people were dying every day, and by the time it was over, some 60 per cent of the population, perhaps a quarter of a million people, were dead. Apart from the human misery this trauma created, it led to a complete economic collapse. Even sixteen years later, in 1672, Naples was still only able to provide a total of half a million ducats for the entire war effort, and its contribution of 120,000 ducats to Milan was a far cry from the 1.3 million Medina de las Torres had been able to send in 1641 [**doc. 27**] (**18**, p. 306). The devastating impact of this plague undermined the power of the Spanish Monarchy at a crucial time when it had become embroiled in war with a new enemy, England.

Philip IV had recognized the English Republic with almost unseemly haste in 1650 and had made every effort to secure a treaty – even, in 1654, indicating his willingness to recognize Cromwell as King (**99**)! But for Cromwell Catholic Spain was 'the natural enemy' who had tried 'to destroy Elizabeth of famous memory' (quoted in **36**, p. 90). Moreover, war with the Spaniards would serve both religion and commerce, 'gain and Godliness'. War did not become 'official' until February 1656, and it went badly for England. The expedition against Hispaniola was a failure and the capture of Jamaica was not regarded as adequate compensation. Moreover, the Dunkirkers were soon disrupting shipping so effectively that a popular jingle urged Cromwell to 'make wars with Dutchmen, peace with Spain, then we shall have money and trade again' (quoted in **44**, p. 34). However, Cromwell preferred to sign a deal with France in 1657 to take Dunkirk.

Yet if the war went badly for England, it was a disaster for Spain. The two silver fleets of 1656 were captured by the English admiral, Robert Blake, and, as a consequence, those which should have sailed in 1657 and 1658 did not do so. This interruption had a damaging effect on Madrid's credit, but even more significant was the disruption of trade and communications created by the English navy off the peninsula, in the Mediterranean and in the English Channel. It effectively cut off the Army of Flanders, and in 1657 Don Juan José wrote from Brussels protesting in the strongest terms over the lack of support. In June 1658 the French army, buttressed by 7,000 English 'ironsides', defeated the Army of Flanders at the battle of the Dunes. Dunkirk was taken in September, along with Ypres and Gravelines, while Turenne advanced to the outskirts of Brussels. In the Mediterranean too the activities of the English navy had effectively cut Italy off from Spain (**20**). All this prompted Philip to state: 'I have always wanted peace and desire it more sincerely every day, and will make any sacrifices on my part for it; the matter, however, depends not on my will but on that of the enemy' (quoted in **52**, p. 209). In fact it was Spain's principal enemy, Cardinal Mazarin, who took the initiative. France was close to bankruptcy* and threatened with internal unrest. Mazarin therefore took advantage of the favourable situation to open negotiations. A truce was signed in May 1659 and a full peace, the Treaty of the Pyrenees, in the following November.

The 124 clauses of the peace were drawn up by Haro and Mazarin on the Isle of Pheasants in the River Bidasoa, which separated the two states. France was confirmed in the possession of Roussillon and Cerdagne (those parts of Catalonia north of the Pyrenees), nearly all of Artois, Gravelines in Flanders (Dunkirk went to England) and a few places in Hainault and Luxemburg. Philip was confirmed in the possession of the rest of the Spanish Netherlands and Franche-Comté. Spanish predominance in Italy was also acknowledged. The French agreed not to aid the Portuguese or the English, and a full pardon was granted to Condé; this was easier for France to swallow now that the prince had been defeated at the battle of the Dunes. In addition, Philip's daughter María Teresa was to marry Louis XIV, though she renounced her right of succession to the Spanish throne – a concession which was made dependent on a dowry of 500,000 gold *escudos* which the Spanish never paid. This marriage would of course have enormous significance for the Spanish succession in the future, as Mazarin had intended. It took place in June 1660 in an elaborate ceremony, again on the Isle of Pheasants.

The Peace of the Pyrenees was a peace of equals. Spanish losses were not great, and France returned some territory and strongholds. With hindsight, historians have regarded the treaty as a symbol of the 'decline of Spain' and the 'ascendancy of France'; 'at the time, however, the Peace of the Pyrenees appeared a far from decisive verdict on the international hierarchy' (**79**, p. 106).

## The end of the reign

It is easy to forget that throughout this period of war against France the Portuguese had been in revolt. Spain had been unable to do very much about this; prior to 1657 only about a million ducats* annually and 12,000 men had been spared for a holding operation on this front (**99**). In 1657 the King decided to use the money earmarked for Flanders, which could not be dispatched because of the English blockade, to attempt the first serious campaign against Portugal since the rebellion had begun. The death of John IV in 1656 and the establishment of a regency government might have seemed like a good opportunity, but the regency proved to be more belligerent than King John had been. The campaign, led by the inexperienced Haro, failed miserably and eventually led to defeat at the battle of Elvas in January 1659. Peace was essential, but for Philip the Portuguese were simply rebels, and once peace had been made with France he intended to bring them to heel.

It is fortunate for Don Luis de Haro that we remember him for the Peace of the Pyrenees and not the Portuguese campaign. He died in 1661, but his eighteen-year ministry, and his personal contribution in particular, are difficult to assess as all his papers were destroyed by fire. What we can say is that he implemented policy with distinctly better results than Olivares. Spain survived 1647–48, made peace with the Dutch, recovered Catalonia, held on to Italy and most of Flanders and made a *paz honesta* with France. It is unfortunate that his achievement was overshadowed by Philip IV's stubborn failure to accept the loss of

Portugal. The problem for Philip was that, despite peace with France, an armistice with the restored Charles II of England in 1660, and an enormous reduction in the Army of Flanders – from 42,000 in 1659, to 11,000 in 1664 – (**71**) he still had no money to fight the Portuguese. Indeed, he was required to declare a partial bankruptcy\* in 1660 to finance the campaign of 1661, and a full bankruptcy in 1662 to finance that of 1663 (**21**). These measures, coming on top of the bankruptcies of 1647 and 1652 (and followed by that of 1666), created a cumulative debt of 221.6 million ducats\* which virtually absorbed the entire free revenue. Spain was now bankrupt in the true sense of the word. This explains why peace with the Dutch and the French did not bring any financial benefit. Only debt repudiation, improved tax collection and/or increased taxation could resolve the problem. However, new taxation could only be granted by the Cortes\*, and its members were reluctant to do this. The last Cortes of Philip IV's reign (1660–64) only granted 1.6 million ducats of the 5 million he requested (**107**).

Philip made the financial situation worse by pouring 5 million ducats per annum into the Portuguese campaign in 1660–65 – more than had been spent on the Army of Flanders at its peak. At the beginning of this period there seemed a good prospect that Spain might be successful, for the Portuguese had lost their French and English allies and were at war with the Dutch. However, peace was made with the Dutch in 1661 and a marriage treaty with Charles II in the same year secured the support of England. Louis XIV gave unofficial help, and the Spanish offensive of 1661–62 was halted. Spain renewed the assault in 1663 but in June the Portuguese army led by Schomberg, a marshal of France, together with 600 French officers and several English regiments, defeated the Spanish at Ameixal. After this battle the Spanish army disintegrated. The Duke of Medina de las Torres, Philip's principal adviser after the death of Haro, advocated peace, but the King was adamant. Another army of 20,000 was scraped together, but this had no better fortune than its predecessors. In June 1665 it was heavily defeated at Vilaviçiosa. In the following September Philip IV died.

Few wept at Philip's passing, for as one of his many critics commented, 'if the King does not die, the kingdom will'. He 'bequeathed to his successor an empty treasury, a discredited currency, and a multitude of new taxes already alienated to financiers' (**63**, p. 171). The crown passed to his 4 -year-old son,

*Descriptive Analysis*

but government was in the hands of Queen Mariana, as regent, guided by the *Junta\* de Gobierno.*

What is remarkable is that Philip IV had anything left to pass on to his son. Despite the strains on the Monarchy, it had survived largely intact, but only by loosening its control. By re-emphasizing local rights and liberties Olivares's successors were able to convince the local elites 'that there were worse fates than subjection to the King of Spain' (**30,** p. 133). 'But there developed a stark contrast between the inert corpse of the Spanish Monarchy and the vigorous government of other European states' (**24**, p. 543), which were attempting to reduce the power of privileged groups and regions. Whereas other nations were forging ahead, Spain was simply hanging on. Sir Richard Fanshaw wrote in 1662: 'the vast increase in power by land and sea which other nations have made upon them since Queen Elizabeth's time hath so altered the balance that Spain must no more pretend to the universal monarchy' (quoted in **83**). In the absence of the old pretender, many were anxious to identify the new one; his name was Louis XIV.

# 6   The Reign of Charles II, 1665–1700

## The regency and Don Juan, 1665–79

The Spanish Monarchy, as has been shown, had great resilience and remained a significant power well into the 1650s. It did admittedly suffer a collapse after 1656, but it had suffered set-backs before, and recovered. What is really significant about the reign of Charles II was this failure to recover. Spain's decline became evident to all, and in particular the decline of Spanish military power. This was not simply because the Spaniards were unable to maintain the sizes of the army and navy they had achieved under Olivares, but because other powers had considerably increased their armed strength. In fact, army sizes in the second half of the seventeenth century doubled, while Spanish forces more than halved.

What Spain lacked after 1665 was strong, clear political direction. Not simply was Charles II only 4 years old when he came to the throne; he was also mentally and physically subnormal and was not expected to live long [**doc. 28**]. Queen Mariana, the Queen Mother (d. 1696), was regent from 1665 to 1675, but Philip IV had ensured that government would be conducted by her in conjunction with a five-man *Junta\* de Gobierno*. Philip's desire for a measure of collective government (the *junta* represented the Church, bureaucracy and the grandees) was in fact a recipe for disaster. An English diplomat reported as early as April 1666 that 'the want of a Minister of State in this government, and the referring of all things to the Council of State, where the power is equal and the animosities very high, breeds infinite delays and irresolution in all affairs' (quoted in **48**, p. 27). However, the really destabilizing aspect of the regency government was the omission of the two most important figures in Spanish politics at the time – namely, the Duke of Medina de las Torres (d. 1668) and Don Juan José, the bastard son of Philip IV. Philip had presumably excluded them because of their opposition to the continuation of the war against Portugal [**doc. 19**].

*Descriptive Analysis*

Philip had left strict instructions to continue the struggle against the Portuguese, and Mariana was true to her husband's wishes. In 1666, 4.5 million ducats* was poured into the campaign, at the cost of yet another bankruptcy* , and the army on the Portuguese front was increased from 20,000 in 1666 to 25,000 in 1667. However, there was no breakthrough and the war remained stalemated. What brought about the recognition of Portuguese independence in 1668 was Louis XIV's attack on the Spanish Netherlands.

The Spanish were taken completely by surprise by the attack, which came in May 1667. Unlike Richelieu and Mazarin, who had spread French forces over a wide variety of fronts, Louis concentrated his 85,000-strong army in one place. The Marquis of Castel Rodrigo, with only 20–30,000 men, could do little other than retreat, leaving garrisons in those fortifications which he felt had a chance of holding out. Louis picked his time well. He himself stated: 'Flanders was short of troops and money; Spain governed by a foreign princess; the Emperor irresolute;... [Habsburg] forces weakened by diverse wars' (quoted in **118**, p. 200). Mariana appointed Don Juan commander-in-chief and governor of the Netherlands with virtual sovereignty. However, the prince was reluctant to take up the appointment; he felt peace should be made with Portugal and, more important, resented his exclusion from government. By setting his demands too high (**63**) he precipitated a crisis in Spain's war effort at a crucial moment, for it prevented Spain from building up its army for the following year. But the failure to confront Louis on the battlefield in 1668 was not only caused by this domestic political crisis; it was also due to the fact that Mariana failed to obtain the support of her brother, the Emperor Leopold I, who was primarily concerned with the question of who would inherit Spain's possessions after Charles II, whose death was thought to be imminent [**doc. 28**]. Although the Emperor Leopold could have expected to inherit the Monarchy *in toto*, he was, by 1667, realistic enough to appreciate that he had to come to some understanding with Louis XIV, who was too strong to ignore. It is against this background that Louis and Leopold negotiated the secret Partition Treaty of January 1668, which they planned to force on Spain by a combination of military and diplomatic pressure. Louis applied the military pressure, by invading and occupying Franche-Comté. Leopold applied the diplomatic pressure. Spain, in fact, had little choice, and Mariana and the Council of State agreed both to the principle of partition and to peace with France at Aix-la-Chapelle.

Louis offered Spain the option of ceding either Franche-Comté or twelve places which formed an enclave in the Spanish Netherlands. To his surprise Mariana's government astutely ceded the twelve places, including Lille and Tournai, in order to frighten the Dutch into giving Spain support (**3**). The Dutch had already formed an alliance with England in January 1668, and the two powers now undertook to 'guarantee' Flanders' borders. It was the Dutch determination to maintain a buffer state between them and France that would in future preserve Madrid's hold on the Spanish Netherlands, rather than Spain's own efforts. As for the Partition Treaty, nothing was signed, for Charles showed no signs of immediate demise. Partition did not, in fact, become a significant issue again until the 1690s.

Throughout the regency (1665–75) and into Charles's majority there was a struggle for power between Mariana and Don Juan José. The bastard prince was politically ambitious and quite popular. The Queen, on the other hand, placed her faith in her Austrian Jesuit confessor, Juan Everard Nithard, who was not popular at all. In 1666 he became Inquisitor General and a member of the *Junta\* de Gobierno*, but he had no power base and was discredited by the foreign-policy humiliations of 1668. Don Juan built up his power base in Catalonia, from where he master-minded a campaign to secure Nithard's dismissal [**doc. 29**]. In January 1669, Don Juan set out for Madrid and civil war seemed a possibility, but the Queen Regent reluctantly agreed to Nithard's expulsion, and to set up a Committee for Reform. Mariana still retained control of government, but her authority had been seriously undermined. Once again Spain was to find itself at war without clear political leadership.

Louis XIV was still determined to take over the Spanish Netherlands, but he was convinced by his advisers that the conquest of Flanders could not occur without first defeating the Dutch (**90**). He launched his attack on them in May 1672, and once again the dramatic progress of Louis's army – 100,000 strong – caused consternation throughout Europe. The Emperor Leopold now changed his mind about neutrality and in August 1673 signed a 'Grand Alliance' with the Dutch and Spain at the Hague. At last Spain had achieved the concrete military backing it had sought for so long. Mariana's government was looking for the restoration of the *status quo* of 1659 and agreed to subsidize both the Dutch and the Austrians. By means of a further sale of *juros\** Spain was able to restore expenditure on the Flanders front to

71

about 3 million ducats* annually, over a third of which now went directly to allies. This was not an abdication of responsibility; it was, on the contrary, the only course open to Madrid if it was to hang on to the Burgundian inheritance. Spain waited to the end of the campaigning season and declared war in September 1673, but any optimism the regency government had soon dissipated. In 1674, Franche-Comté was overrun by French troops (and was, as it turned out, lost for good), rebellion broke out in Messina in Sicily, and Louis even invaded Catalonia, albeit with a small force.

Mariana had come to place her faith in Don Fernando Valenzuela, considered by many to be an upstart *hidalgo**, and in 1675 he was created a marquis. In the same year Charles attained his fourteenth birthday and officially came of age. This marked the official end of the regency, but Charles was never to be a significant force. The papal nuncio said of him: 'he is weak in body as in mind. Now and then he gives signs of intelligence, memory and a certain liveliness; usually he shows himself slow and indifferent, torpid and indolent. One can do with him what one wishes because he lacks his own will' (quoted in **52**, p. 258). Although the regency was terminated, the *Junta**, under the Queen's presidency, continued for two more years, and it was a measure of the Queen's confidence that she was able to recall Valenzuela (who had been temporarily dismissed) in 1676. In June he was made Master of the Horse; in July he was made chief gentleman of the bedchamber with precedence over all other nobles; and in November he was given control of the government as 'prime minister', and lodged in the Alcázar palace (**48**). The meteoric rise of this upstart caused consternation among the aristocracy and a major political crisis. In a gesture reminiscent of the time of Olivares the grandees simply went on strike. On 15 December 1676 twenty-four of them issued a manifesto denouncing the Queen Mother and Valenzuela and calling on Don Juan to take over government. Under this pressure the Queen Mother's government crumbled and Don Juan was summoned. In January 1677 the prince arrived at the head of an army of 15,000, offering his services to Charles II.

Don Juan exiled the Queen Mother to Toledo, and Valenzuela to the Philippines, at the same time as he rewarded his followers with honours in an attempt to build up his power base [**doc. 30**]. By the summer, however, complaints against the government were mounting. A satirical paper asked: 'Are there less taxes? Less *donativos**? Has the price of food come down? Have the fleets been repaired? Have we lost less in war? Are the prospects better that the people will be relieved, the kingdom saved and our condition improved?' (quoted in **63**, p. 373). The harvest of 1677 was a disaster and the situation in 1678 was even worse, with inflation reaching its highest point and an outbreak of the plague. Once again the government had no money, for the aristocracy would not respond to Don Juan's request for a *donativo*, and he was forced in the autumn of 1678 to make concessions at the Peace of Nijmegen.

Spain was very much the victim at the Peace of Nijmegen, but matters could have been far worse. Although Spain lost Franche-Comté and some fifteen towns in Flanders (as well as Haiti), Don Juan could point to the fact that France had restored Ghent, Courtrai, Oudenarde, Louvain and the Duchy of Limburg, and had withdrawn from Sicily and Catalonia (**91**). In effect, Louis had abandoned his aim of conquering the Spanish Netherlands. The new relationship with France was consummated in 1679 with the marriage of Charles II to Marie Louise of Orléans, the niece of Louis XIV. However, Don Juan's direction of policy did not last long; in July 1679 he was taken ill with a fever and died, aged 50. There was little display of remorse at the death of this once popular prince, though he had laid the foundations for the reform of the administration, the economy and the currency (see below).

## Crisis and reform, 1676–91

In the decade after 1676 'Castilians were visited by scourges of biblical proportions' (**63**, p. 393). Heavy rains in southern Spain ruined the harvest in 1677, while drought ruined the crops in the following two years. Flooding and hail in northern Spain between 1679 and 1681 destroyed crops there, while drought struck again in the south in the years 1682–83 [**doc. 31**]. Heavy rain fell again in 1683–84, and in 1685 there was severe drought in Galicia. In 1687 locusts swept over Catalonia – 'people were stunned . . . it was as if the end of the world had come', observed a contemporary (quoted in **52**, p. 270). Malnutrition made the population suscep-tible to epidemic disease, and although the plague in fact pre-ceded the natural disasters, it was sustained by them. It was not as vicious as previous epidemics, and it did not halt the demographic upturn which had begun in the 1660s, but it was more prolonged. All these disasters quite naturally had a devastating effect on the Castilian economy and on the government's tax revenues.

The most pressing problems facing the government were the cumulative *juro**  debt and monetary instability. At the beginning of the reign the *juro* debt was swallowing up at least 75 per cent of revenue, and in 1678 the Council of Finance reported that 'all the revenue has been applied to *juros* and other payments, leaving nothing with which to meet the many pressing expenses that arise daily' (quoted in **48**, p. 367). Inflation was also a serious problem, for prices in Castile were sky high, and the French ambassador estimated that goods cost twice as much in Madrid as elsewhere. In 1665, the premium on silver was 115 per cent; it rose to 175 per cent in 1670 and 275 per cent by 1680. Thus to send 1 million ducats* in silver to the Netherlands cost the government 3,750,000 ducats in *vellón** coinage. It was decided in 1679 that a massive deflation was the only solution and the decree was issued on 10 February 1680, only a few months after Don Juan José's death. *Vellón* was revalued at 25 per cent of its face value and the premium on silver was reduced from 275 per cent to 50 per cent. This was accompanied by a decree in November 1680 fixing prices at an artificially low level. 'The combination of deflation and price control produced a price collapse unparalleled in Spanish history' (**63**, p. 397): 50 per cent in two years. This caused widespread panic and dismay, for the old coinage could not be used until restamped, and whole communities suddenly found themselves without cash. Barter became common, and thousands lost their savings. The contemporary historian Antonio de Solís wrote that the measure 'has totally destroyed trade and private fortunes. No one uses money. . . . Everywhere there is poverty and bankruptcy' (quoted in **48**, p. 365). It also led to a reduction in tax revenue.

Such a dramatic deflation could have only taken place at a time of peace. Charles II continued Don Juan's foreign policy of *rapprochement* with France, no doubt encouraged by the new Queen, Marie Louise, who appears to have quickly superseded the Queen Mother in Charles's affections. But the maintenance of peace was threatened when Louis XIV set up special courts, called chambers of reunion, to determine what were dependencies of the territories ceded to France since 1648 and to 'reunite' them. A series of dubious legal judgments enabled Louis to claim more of the Spanish Netherlands and almost all of Spanish Luxemburg, which he blockaded in November 1681. This intimidation enabled William of Orange to reconstitute the alliance of 1673; he signed a treaty with the Emperor in February 1682 and with Spain in May. In September 1683 Louis's forces entered the Spanish Netherlands, and in December Spain declared war. The Spaniards were hoping for assistance from the Emperor in the aftermath of his victory over the Turks at Vienna, but in this they were disappointed, for Leopold's priority was to pursue the defeated Turkish army. William of Orange, also, let the Spaniards down, for although he sent 10,000 men to aid them he was unable to persuade the Dutch burghers to engage in another war. Spain was therefore left to fight France alone.

The significance of the brief war of 1683–84 is that it demonstrated how far France had progressed since the 1640s and how far Spanish military power had declined. Even if the Spanish Monarchy had been able to maintain the levels of recruitment of the 1630s, which it could not, it would have been no match for the France of Louis XIV. Louis had a peacetime standing army of 200,000 men consisting of a number of operational armies of about 60,000 each (**95**). The Army of Flanders, by contrast, contained a mere 20,000 men, the Army of Milan 10,000, and the garrison of Luxemburg 3,000 (**32**). Unlike in 1667 when Louis concentrated his forces on one front, he was now able to strike at the Spanish on three; in Flanders, in Luxemburg and in Catalonia. It was no contest, and by June 1684 Luxemburg and the County of Flanders had been taken. Having obtained his objective, and not wishing to provoke a wider war, Louis offered terms, and since Madrid and Vienna would not agree to a full peace, the twenty-year Truce of Regensburg, confirming Louis's gains to that point (including Luxemburg and the County of Flanders) was signed on 15 August 1684 (**118**). It was Louis's aim to turn this into a full peace; it was the aim of Madrid and Vienna to reverse it. In 1686, therefore, Spain joined the Dutch and the Emperor in the League of Augsburg, which aimed to prevent further French expansion.

In the wake of the military humiliation of 1684 the Count of Oropesa became chief minister. Oropesa impressed contemporaries, and this judgment has been echoed by subsequent historians, but his achievements did not match his intentions. However, during his term as prime minister (1685–91) he attempted to reform the finances, the Church and the bureaucracy. Of necessity he revived the campaign against *juros**. Decrees of 1685 and 1687 cut the number of them by 50–75 per cent, and reduced interest rates from 5 per cent to 4 per cent. In order to ameliorate the impact of the savage devaluation of 1680, silver was devalued by about 20 per cent by a decree of October 1686. This was in effect an inflationary measure, 'but a sound and justified one' (**63**, p. 400). Silver came back into circulation, prices recovered and the government abolished or reduced many *sisas** to help matters. But

75

the problem of inadequate revenue remained acute. Because the government had been too weak to call the Cortes*, no new taxation had been possible since 1664 and many existing taxes had been reduced. The Marquis of Los Vélez, president of the *Hacienda* (treasury), estimated in 1687 that revenue was only 8.4 million *escudos*, while commitments for the coming year amounted to 12.3 million. Accordingly, a decree in February 1688 stated that the government would in future pre-empt 4.7 million *escudos* for its immediate requirements; preferential *juros* and other expenses could be met only from what was left. In 1690 the government actually pre-empted 4.5 million *escudos* [**doc. 2**]. This policy was a sound (and necessary) arrangement, and it was coupled with the cancellation of arrears. But it did not tackle the problem of the cumulative *juro* debt, which stood in the way of the government's aim of solvency. Instead of tinkering with the debt the government ought to have repudiated it. However, so many institutions and individuals – widows, hospitals, merchants, bankers, townspeople, nobles, clergy, monasteries – had a vested interest in the continuation of the system that its abolition was not practical politics. Even tinkering led to considerable dissatisfaction, and did little for Oropesa's popularity. When we consider that Louis XIV was able to spend anything between 30 and 60 million ducats* annually, Spain's provision of 4.7 million looks paltry indeed. And paltry it was: if we look at the budget for 1690 [**doc. 2**] we can see that there was no provision for the Army of Flanders, no provision for the navy – indeed, no provision for proper peacetime defence. Moreover, there was clearly no possibility of making provision for fighting a war, as became apparent in the 1690s.

Given this dire situation, it is not surprising that Oropesa should have sought to increase income and reduce expenditure. Although he had little success, he did manage to persuade Rome to authorize an increased revenue from the clergy, and he initiated a campaign against the excessive number of clerics and false vocations. As well as too many clerics, the Monarchy was also encumbered with too many bureaucrats. The administration had become bloated, for as well as the *letrados*\* there were the more numerous *capa y espada* (cloak and sword) bureaucrats; that is, nobles who had purchased their position or had received it by way of royal favour, and were often paid prior to assuming office, or even *in absentia*. As the councils were increasingly filled with people who lacked competence, they spent more and more of their time on disputes over their jurisdictions. In order to reduce conciliar numbers, Oropesa issued a decree suppressing the purchase of offices in 1687, and in 1691 membership of the councils was actually reduced. Unfortunately the effectiveness of these measures was undermined by Oropesa's fall from power in that year. Attempts to reduce the cost of the royal household were unsuccessful; in fact between 1680 and 1690 costs rose 50 per cent because of the need to provide for three royal personages – the King, the Queen and the Queen Mother. Oropesa had more success cutting pensions and *mercedes\**, which virtually constituted 'a welfare service for the aristocracy'(**63**, p. 356) [**doc. 32**]. Some were stopped, others were abolished and all were taxed (excepting widows and veterans). Expenses in this area fell from 1.5 million *escudos* in 1680 to just over 600,000 in 1690 (**48**).

Despite membership of the League of Augsburg, Spain remained neutral when France became involved in war against the Emperor and the Dutch in 1688. As long as Queen Marie Louise was alive, relations with France remained relatively good, but in March 1689 she died in circumstances suggesting poison. The Queen Mother and the Austrian faction now gained full ascendancy over Charles II, and Louis XIV reacted by declaring war the following month. Six months later Charles II was married to Mariana of Pfalz-Neuburg, the Emperor Leopold's sister-in-law, and in June 1690 Spain joined the Treaty of Vienna, thereby re-establishing the alliance with the Emperor and with William of Orange, who was now also King William III of England. Oropesa did not long survive all these changes. The Queen Mother, Mariana, and the new Queen (also Mariana) combined with the grandees to have him dismissed in 1691. By threatening the aristocracy with taxation, the Church with reform, and the bureaucracy with reduction, he had alienated the most powerful sectors of society, and once he lost the support of the King (or rather the Queen) his position was untenable. With him went all the impetus for reform.

## War, faction and succession, 1690–1700

After Oropesa's fall Charles II did not appoint a prime minister, but decided to govern himself. 'In those first days he dedicated himself with unbelievable application to the management of affairs; but early enthusiasm was followed by the weariness occasioned by ill health, and he referred matters to many and different ministers' (quoted in **48**, p. 375). The result was chaos.

*Descriptive Analysis*

Real power was appropriated by Queen Mariana, who filled the Council of State with her own clients and provided positions for a number of her German advisers, at the same time placating the Spanish aristocracy by giving them titles [**doc. 30**] and pensions. Yet if the Queen controlled the court and patronage, no one seemed to control the government. Stanhope, the British ambassador, complained in 1694: 'This country is in a most miserable condition; no head to govern, and every man in office does what he pleases, without fear of being called to account' (quoted in **63**, p. 420). At this time it appears the Queen Mother had gained the upper hand, for she persuaded the King to draw up a will in favour of the son of the Elector of Bavaria (see below). In December 1694, the Council of Castile complained of the German influence in the government, and in January 1695, Archbishop Portocarrero presented to the King a strongly worded request that 'these people (*esa gente*) leave Your Majesty's dominions' (quoted in **48**, p. 389), but although there were some changes the German party continued in power. With the death of the Queen Mother, Mariana of Austria, in 1696, the Queen's influence over the King became supreme. Yet still the government was without effective leadership. It was also without cash.

'Throughout the 1690s the Spanish government existed in a state of what can suitably be called permanent bankruptcy*' (**48**, p. 387). The reform of 1688, although assuring the crown a minimum income, had made no provision for financing a war, and a special committee was set up to deal with the problem once Spain became involved in hostilities. This decreed in 1692 that payment of all state debts up to 1690 be suspended, except those affecting the royal household and the war. This decree had some effect, but even so the government was never able to apply more than a few million ducats* per year to the war effort. So bad was the situation that in 1695 the government sold the viceroyalties of Mexico and Peru to the highest bidders. It is hardly surprising, given the Spanish Monarchy's bankruptcy and lack of effective government, that its war effort should have been pathetic. Nor is it surprising that the Monarchy came to resemble a pawn in the hands of other powers. It was in the 1690s that Spain lost control of its destiny.

Louis XIV had not wanted this war and he missed an opportunity to take Catalonia in 1689 when there was considerable peasant discontent and the Spanish army was wholly unprepared. This enabled the Spaniards to build up their forces, and by 1690 an army of 14,000 was in place in Catalonia. In Flanders the Spanish garrisons were stripped so that a field army of 30,000 could be found, and this joined with the Dutch army of 70,000 under the overall command of their general, the Count of Waldeck-Pyrmont. In July 1690 Pyrmont decided to take on a larger French army at Fleurus but he was defeated and forced to withdraw. This was the last pitched battle of the war in which Spanish troops fought in defence of the Spanish Netherlands (17, p. 239), and in 1691 William III insisted on the removal of the Spanish governor and his replacement by Max Emmanuel of Bavaria. By 1693 forces in this theatre exceeded 100,000 on each side, but the Spanish role was negligible. Indeed Stanhope commented: 'Flanders they [the Spanish] look upon as being our concern rather than theirs' (quoted in 95, p. 195). A similar situation developed in Milan where the bulk of the 40,000-strong army was manned and administered by the Austrians, since Naples was no longer able to supply the men and money it had done fifty years before.

Only in Catalonia did Spain play the leading role (as indeed it should have done), yet this was where the French made the most headway. Although Spanish forces in this theatre were reinforced by three German regiments sent by the Emperor in 1695, they could not hold off the French assault indefinitely, and on 10 August 1697 Barcelona fell. Charles II announced his intention to go to the Catalan front, but fortunately this was not necessary, as the major powers had decided to make peace. In September 1697 agreement was reached at Ryswick. Louis was extremely generous to Spain, agreeing to return the County of Flanders and Luxemburg, and evacuate Catalonia. He was acting on the assumption that Charles II was near to death, and that it was essential for him to establish good relations with Madrid, if France was to have any chance of gaining from the Spanish succession.

The question of who would succeed Charles II became the major political issue of the 1690s, particularly since he was now frequently unwell and would obviously have no children of his own. After the war ended in 1697 there began a period of intense diplomatic manoeuvring in Madrid and elsewhere (38). Already because of the war the Emperor had his nominee in control in Flanders, large forces in Milan and several German regiments within Spain. However, Louis XIV was not going to allow everything to go to the Austrian Habsburgs. He sent one of his soldiers, the Marquis d'Harcourt, to be his ambassador to Spain and to warn the Spanish: 'I have thirty battalions and three thousand cavalry placed in a manner so that they could assemble quickly if it becomes necessary' (quoted in **118**, p. 495). The arrival of Harcourt in Madrid in 1698 'was the whole turning point in the saga of the succession' (**48** p. 386). In April 1698 Cardinal Portocarrero, hitherto pro-Bavarian, committed himself to the French cause, and a French party with some solid support emerged, despite the fact that the pro-Austrian Oropesa had been recalled as prime minister in March. Louis expected the Monarchy to be willed to Vienna, and therefore proposed partition, discussing the matter with William III, whom he thought would be more open to persuasion on this issue. In October William and Louis signed the first Partition Treaty, which left the bulk of the Monarchy to the Elector of Bavaria's son, Joseph Ferdinand, a great grandson of Philip IV. However, Milan was to go to Archduke Charles (Leopold's second son) and Naples, Sicily, the Italian coastal forts and the Basque province of Guipuzcoa to Louis's heir, the Dauphin Louis. When they learnt of the treaty, Leopold was furious and Queen Mariana broke the furniture in her room (**86**). Charles II reacted by (once again) leaving his inheritance in its entirety to Joseph Ferdinand (November 1698), but the latter's death in February 1699 led to a whole new round of negotiations.

Serious bread riots in Madrid in April 1699 severely damaged the Austrian faction, as they were directed against Oropesa's government and the Queen. Charles sent Oropesa into exile in May, and control of government passed to Cardinal Portocarrero of the French faction. After a considerable amount of negotiation, a Second Partition Treaty was finalized by France and the maritime powers in March 1700. This proposed giving Spain, the overseas empire and the Spanish Netherlands to Archduke Charles, while the dauphin Louis was to have the Italian lands. However, there was little chance of this being accepted in either Vienna or Madrid. When the Council of State met on 6 June 1700, its principal concern was to maintain the integrity of the Monarchy. In Spain the idea that the Monarchy could be preserved from partition only by the power of France was gaining ground. Leaving it entirely to the Emperor Leopold would lead to French invasion and partition. Yet on the other hand, leaving it to France might simply lead to the implementation of the Partition Treaty. In other words, partition seemed inevitable either way. In a final attempt to avert this, the King decided on 2 October 1700 to leave all the Spanish dominions to the Duke of Anjou, Louis's grandson, on condition that the crowns of Spain and France should never be united in one person.

If this was not acceptable to Louis, then the entire Monarchy was to be offered to Leopold's second son, the Archduke Charles [**doc. 33**]. Charles II had taken his decision just in time, for a month later, on 1 November 1700, the last of the Spanish Habsburgs died.

The will of Charles II took Europe by surprise. Even Louis XIV seemed unprepared, despite intelligence from Rome. To the astonishment of the Spanish ambassador, his immediate response to the offer of twenty-two crowns was simply 'we shall see' (quoted in **118**). But after sleeping on it, and bearing in mind that it was to be offered to Vienna if he refused, he accepted on behalf of his grandson. On 16 November 1700, Louis introduced Anjou to the court as Philip V of Spain. He was accepted by the governors of Flanders and Milan but not by the Emperor Leopold, who responded to this unwelcome news by sending troops to Italy. Philip V reached Madrid in February 1701 amid popular acclaim and optimism that the new ruling house would bring a revival of Spain's fortunes.

What can we say in conclusion about the reign of Charles II? There were undoubtedly financial reforms – namely, the stabilization of the currency, the elimination of inflation, and the reduction of taxation. Bullion shipments from America achieved their highest figures ever [**doc. 8**] and the population began to grow again, after years of crisis [**doc. 7**]. In addition, agricultural output, wool production and cloth manufacture all increased. All of these factors undoubtedly contributed to the revival of Spanish power in the eighteenth century, but as a refutation of the conventional and unfavourable verdict on the reign of Charles, they are 'not entirely convincing' (**26**). For one thing, they have to be put in perspective. They were recovery from losses and sometimes not even that. For instance, Segovian cloth production did revive but it was still, in 1700, only one-third what it had been pre-1630 (**105**). Although the population recovered, the whole peninsula probably numbered only 6–7 million in the 1680s, down 2 million from 1600, and less than one-third the population of France. Bullion shipments undoubtedly did recover, but the royal share declined from 30 per cent earlier in the century to half that by mid-century and to as little as 4 per cent in Charles's reign. Therefore the government did not get the benefit. Moreover, the financial reforms led to chaos, and reducing taxes did nothing to alleviate the cumulative debt or enable the Monarchy to pay its soldiers.

The government was so weak that it did not benefit from the economic upturn. What Spain needed more than anything else was effective monarchy, but observers were pessimistic about the practicality of changing the situation. The French envoy, the Count of Rebenec, observed in 1689:

> If one looks closely at the government of this monarchy, one will find it in excessive disorder, but in the state it is in, it is scarcely possible to bring about change without exposing it to dangers more to be feared than the evil itself. A total revolution would be necessary before perfect order could be established in this state. (quoted in **110**, p. 95)

In the *ancien régime* the role of the monarch was so important that his own character often had a decisive influence on the course of events. It was especially important in the case of the Spanish Monarchy because the King was the entire *raison d'être* for the regime. A retarded king retarded the entire structure, and it is perhaps surprising that Charles II was not 'replaced'. It may seem simplistic to attribute Spanish weakness to the failure of government, but the succeeding reign of Philip V was to demonstrate that, given better leadership, Spain had the potential to revive.

## Postscript: the War of the Spanish Succession, 1702–14

Charles's will was designed to prevent partition, but partition is exactly what happened. Leopold did not accept the will and Louis XIV provoked the maritime powers into taking up the Habsburg cause. The anti-Bourbon alliance was forged by fear of a new universal monarchy; it was felt that the union of France and Spain would create 'a super power, a trade monopoly and a protected market' (**62**, p. 23). The Spanish Monarchy had been willed to the Bourbons in the hope that the power of Louis XIV would protect it. However, in this war, for the first time, Louis suffered a series of catastrophic set-backs. Defeat at the battle of Blenheim in 1704 put him on the defensive and by 1705 he was prepared to concede partition. In 1706, the Franco-Spanish position deteriorated even further, as defeats at Ramillies and Turin drove the Bourbons from the Spanish Netherlands and Spanish Italy respectively. Spain itself became subject to foreign invasion and civil war, for when the Archduke Charles, 'Charles III', arrived in the peninsula in 1705, Valencia and Catalonia rose up and declared for him. Castile, however, remained loyal to Philip V, and despite the brief occupation of Madrid by the enemy in 1706, the new Bourbon King was not defeated.

By 1708–9, after further set-backs at Oudenarde and Malplaquet, Philip's principal backer, Louis XIV, was ready for peace even at the cost of abandoning Philip V. But he would not accept the allied demand that he should forcibly eject his grandson from Spain, and the war therefore continued. In 1710, however, the Tories came to power in Britain, ready to compromise, and in 1711 'Charles III' became the Emperor Charles VI. This represented a strengthening of Habsburg power that none of the allies had sought, and partition of the Spanish inheritance once again became the objective. Anglo-French discussions in 1711 settled many of the issues, but the terms were not finalized until 1713, when the Treaty of Utrecht was signed. Great Britain received Gibraltar, Minorca (captured in 1704 and 1708 respectively) and the *asiento** (the rights to the slave trade); the Dutch gained protective barrier fortresses in the Netherlands, and Victor Amadeus of Savoy was given Sicily. Philip V was confirmed in his possession of Spain and the overseas empire (Spanish America had remained loyal to Philip throughout), but he renounced his claims to the French succession. Charles VI of Austria was to receive the Spanish Netherlands, Milan, Naples, Sardinia and the Italian fortresses. This was the subject of a separate agreement between France and Austria, the Treaty of Rastatt, in 1714. There was no agreement signed between Spain and the Emperor.

The Catalans, who were effectively abandoned at Utrecht, elected to fight on alone, but after Philip V took Barcelona in 1714 they had to accept the inevitable. Philip had already reconquered Aragon and Valencia, whose *fueros** he abolished in 1707. Now in 1716, the *fueros* of Catalonia went the same way. Customs barriers between the constituent kingdoms were removed, and a single comprehensive tax was introduced. For the first time in its history Spain became a unitary, national state with an effective central government, greater revenue (which nearly doubled between 1703 and 1713, from about 11 million ducats* to about 20 million), and better armed forces (the size of the army quadrupled between 1703 and 1722) (**46, 62**). This achievement clearly demonstrates what strong and purposeful leadership could achieve, even in a country that seemed beyond hope of redemption.

# Part Three:   Assessment

## 7   The Decline of Spain?

Since Henry Kamen's controversial article entitled the 'Decline of Spain: A Historical Myth' appeared in 1978 (**47**), it has become less fashionable to talk of Spain's decline. Prior to this, the concept was well established. It began with contemporaries (**30**, ch. 11); González de Cellorigo, writing in 1600, spoke of *declinación*, and in 1640 Jerónimo Fernández de Mata wrote, 'it is said that when empires reach their peak, they begin to decline' (quoted in **51**). But both were writing in years of disaster (plague and revolt, respectively) and the pessimism of the *arbitristas** in general was not always a fair reflection of reality. However, by the nineteenth century the idea that Spain had declined from the reign of Philip III onwards was well established, and historical explanations (for example, Ranke and Hume) usually emphasized the ignorance, sloth and clericalism of Spanish society and the weakness of the Spanish kings. This interpretation received an economic dimension in 1938 with the publication of Earl Hamilton's famous article (**34**) and in the 1950s with work by the Chaunus (**16**). However, as Professor Elliott pointed out in his 1961 article (**30**, ch. 10), these fiscal and commercial studies were limited to external influences (that is, American silver) on the Spanish economy, and took insufficient account of internal economic conditions. He emphasized the importance of the internal demographic and agrarian crises between 1590 and 1620 but went on to make the clear distinction between the economic decline of Castile and the decline of Spanish political power. The latter he placed in 1640 with the loss of hegemony. Thus there were two types of decline, and the economic preceded the political.

Dr Kamen did not dispute the political decline of the Spanish Monarchy; in his 1978 article he stated, 'we cannot question the obvious fact that there was a decline in imperial and military power' (**47**, p. 32). His concern was with the thesis of economic 'decline', though the title of his article, as well as a number of subsequent statements (**50**, pp. 4 and 61–2) can be a little misleading if this distinction is not understood. Moreover, he focused his attention on the kingdoms of Castile and Aragon. He was not concerned, in his article at least, with Portugal, Naples, Sicily, Milan and so on, though ten years later he was prepared to concede more importance to Spanish Italy (**50**, p. 6). In fact the scope of the article was a lot narrower than the title implied.

The gist of Dr Kamen's thesis is that Spain (namely, Aragon and Castile) could not decline economically because 'Spain never rose' (**47**, p. 25). In other words, since Spain had never been an economically strong nation it could not have declined 'before ever becoming rich' (**47**, p. 35). Professor Israel took issue with this contention in an article in 1981 (**39**). He pointed out that contemporaries – the *arbitristas** – were very aware of a sense of economic decline, 'a sudden shift, an abrupt economic contraction' (**39**, p. 171). He also pointed out that there had been considerable industrial growth in the sixteenth century, particularly in textiles, which was abruptly reversed in the first two decades of the seventeenth century. Depopulation too was sudden, occurring in the period 1595–1621. As for Kamen's assertion that there was no agreement about the timing of the so-called decline, Israel contended that 'there is today a growing body of opinion which clearly discerns the beginning of [economic] decline during the early years of the reign of Philip III and the completion of the process during the middle decades of the seventeenth century' (**39**, p. 180).

Dr Kamen is right to stress the basic weaknesses of the Spanish economy and the cyclical nature of economic activity. He is right to suggest that agrarian depression and trade fluctuation were part of an international pattern (though Castile and Naples were particularly hard hit), and he has a point when he states that unrelated phenomena – plague, military defeat, trade depression – have been 'jumbled together' (**47**, p. 48), for in fact no precise connections have been established. But to suggest, as he still did in 1988, that 'the concept of "decline", in effect, is no longer used by working historians, as a guide to what really happened in early modern Spain' (**50**, pp. 61–2) is patently not true. We have to ask ourselves why Professor Elliott, an acknowledged expert in this field, affirmed in 1983 that 'there seems no good reason to contest the established view that this [that is, the seventeenth century] was the century of Spain's decline' (**30**, p. 266) and why Professor Parker, another distinguished historian of the period, pointedly entitled his 1984 bibliographical essay in *History Today*, 'The Decline of Spain' (**76**).

*Assessment*

The answer, of course, is that Spain (Castile and its territories) *did* decline, economically and politically. Why then have Dr Kamen's views had such an impact? The answer must be because we are not really sure about the precise relationship between the economic decline and the political decline. This is because the economic decline preceded the political one by some considerable time; moreover, during the course of this economic decline the Spanish Monarchy showed remarkable resilience, generating greater tax revenues and assembling larger forces than ever before. Too much focus on economic decline can blind us to the achievement of political survival, something that was recognized by both Professor Elliott and Dr Stoye in the 1960s (**24**, **91**). More recently Dr Stradling has pointed out that the 'orthodox, economics-centred schema for the "decline of Spain", though containing much validity in its own right, is no longer' a sufficient explanation (**93**).

Let us just remind ourselves of the main features of economic decline (see Chapter 2). There was demographic loss from about 1580, and no recovery until the 1660s; however actual losses were not made good until the eighteenth century. The populations of Castile and Naples hit bottom in the 1650s. There was a reduction in agricultural output by as much as one-third, with recovery in Castile and Naples only taking place in the 1680s and 1690s. Spanish industrial output declined, particularly from the 1620s, and here there was no recovery. Trade also declined from the 1620s, bullion shipments hit bottom in the 1650s, and the American trade continued to fall. Although a general economic recovery was under way by the end of the seventeenth century, the crisis was both relatively intense and relatively long-term in those key areas of the Spanish Monarchy, Castile and Naples.

A decline in the numbers of the taxpaying population and an overall decline in the wealth generated by the economy at a time when the government was taking on new commitments and seeking new and more taxation was clearly a recipe for disaster. What is remarkable is that Olivares was able to increase taxation in the 1630s and build up Spanish forces to unprecedented numbers. However, his policy of spreading the burden beyond Castile threatened to undermine the entire political structure of the Monarchy. Moreover, because tax revenue was insufficient the debt grew prodigiously – from 85 million ducats* in 1598 to 221 million in 1667. The government paid for defence in the present by mortgaging the future. The link between economic and political decline was not only the growth in the debt, but also the growth in arrears in taxation that began to build up from the 1630s. People simply could not afford to pay. By 1649 it was estimated that Castile as a whole owed 36 million ducats in arrears. This is the background to the dramatic collapse of Spanish power at the end of Philip IV's reign.

It has been the theme of this Seminar Study that the Spanish Monarchy was an amalgam of great strengths and weaknesses; it had wealth and population but it was politically disparate, geographically dispersed and expensive to run. The eclipse of France during the period 1559–1629 and the slow pace of its recovery thereafter enabled Spain to enjoy a period of hegemony in Europe. However, Philip II (1556–98), in fighting the Dutch, the English and the French, became disastrously overcommitted and put an enormous strain on the financial resources of Castile which bore the main burden. The much maligned Duke of Lerma (in office *c.* 1598–*c.* 1618) restored a sense of proportion to Spanish policy by making peace with the English (1604), a truce with the Dutch (1609), a marriage alliance with France (from 1611), and by reorienting Spanish policy towards the Mediterranean. However, despite the fact that Spanish power and influence achieved new heights under Philip III (1598–1621), there is no doubt that the economic downturn and the abandonment of a forward policy by Lerma led many contemporaries to believe that Spain was losing its grip, that Spain was in decline. Olivares (in office 1622–43) offered the combination of domestic reform with a return to the forward policy of Philip II, but warfare killed reform and put an inordinate strain on an already fragile entity. His success in extending the tax burden (particularly in Castile and Naples) and in increasing Spain's military capacity was offset by setbacks in Mantua (1628–31) and the Netherlands (particularly 1629–32 and 1637–39) and by open war with France (from 1635). Moreover, the obsession with the preservation of *reputación** at all costs meant that opportunities for peace and retrenchment were missed. The revolts of Catalonia and Portugal in 1640, and of Naples and Sicily in 1647 marked the end of the period of Spanish hegemony, but they did not signal the collapse of Spain nor its eclipse by France. In the 1650s the Monarchy enjoyed a brief revival and a balance of power was maintained.

However, Spanish power did collapse dramatically between the years 1656 and 1668. War with England deprived the Monarchy of bullion and cut its communications with Italy and Flanders.

Moreover, English soldiers at the battle of the Dunes (1658) ensured a French victory and tipped the scales in the latter's favour after ten years of stalemate. The devastating plague in Naples in 1656, coming on top of the revolt in 1647, deprived the Monarchy of the financial and manpower resources of what had become Spain's most important source of strength after Castile, and the war with Portugal continued to drain the treasury. By the 1660s Spanish finances were in a chaotic state; the combination of the cumulative *juro** debt and the growth of arrears led to a succession of bankruptcies* in 1647, 1652, 1660 (partial), 1662 and 1666, which completely destroyed the government's credit and eliminated the possibility of future large-scale borrowing. What revenue the government did receive was, technically, swallowed up by the interest payments on the cumulative debt. By the late 1650s Spain's weak condition had convinced the Duke of Medina de las Torres that peace and retrenchment were essential [**doc. 21**]. At the same time, France was increasing in strength, and Louis XIV was determined to bring the Spanish Habsburgs down. Under Colbert tax revenue was doubled, while Le Tellier and Louvois were busy turning the French army into the most powerful and cohesive force in Europe (**89**). The change in status was signalled in the war of 1667–68. Louis proved to be Spain's nemesis, initially as predator and later as protector.

Spanish fortunes had dipped before; what was different after 1668 was that there was no recovery. The financial situation did not improve; tax collection remained problematical, the debt increased, no new taxes were introduced, no large-scale borrowing was possible, and revenue actually declined. The numbers in the armed forces were allowed to run down to a mere 50,000 in the 1690s, compared with 170,000 in the 1630s – and this at a time when France had over 400,000 men under arms. Spain became a puppet in the international arena, saved only by the Dutch and Austrians. And yet the Spanish economy was recovering, as the population began to grow and agrarian output and livestock numbers increased, in Spanish Italy as well as the Iberian peninsula. Even if we place this recovery in perspective – losses were not made good until well into the eighteenth century – we cannot escape the conclusion that failure to recover and translate this economic upturn into increased tax revenue was largely a failure of government (Chapter 6). Throughout the period 1665 to 1700 the Spanish Monarchy was without clear leadership or direction.

It would be simplistic to claim that a revived Spanish Monarchy under a strong king could have led to a restoration of Spanish hegemony; for one thing, the Monarchy's disparate population of *c.* 15 million was no match for France's 20 million under the strong leadership of Louis XIV. But Spain's military and naval revival under the Bourbons, between 1713 and 1748, which led to the reconquest of Sardinia, Sicily and Naples, suggests that much more might have been possible in Charles II's reign, given a different ruler. Of course the real catastrophe did not come between 1656 and 1668, or even later during the King's majority, but in and after 1700 with the death of Charles II, with invasion and ultimately partition. Just as Spain's rise had been brought about by dynastic inheritance so its demise was brought about by the end of the dynasty. Although counter-factual speculation has little validity in general, in this case there are grounds for suggesting that had Charles II had a healthy son, Spain's political decline, like its economic decline, might have only been cyclical.

# Part Four:   Documents

## Income and expenditure, 1621–40

*Hacienda income, 1621–40* (%)

| | |
|---|---|
| From Cortes* of Castile (*servicios**) | 38.0 |
| From Cortes of crown of Aragon | 1.1 |
| From Spanish Church (Three Graces) | 15.6 |
| Bullion from Indies, 1621–39 | 9.5 |
| Discounts on and sale of *juros** | 9.0 |
| Re-coinages | 7.5 |
| *Donativos**, 1624– 35 | 5.5 |
| Sales of office, vassals, etc. | 3.5 |
| Salt tax | 2.9 |
| *Media anata** | 1.3 |
| Seizure of private bullion | 1.2 |
| Other | 4.9 |

Total 237.3 million ducats*

*Hacienda expenditure, 1621–40*

| | |
|---|---|
| *Asientos** and bankers (i.e., military and debts) | 70.4 |
| Mediterranean fleet | 5.3 |
| Atlantic fleet | 4.5 |
| Forts and frontiers | 3.7 |
| Army in Spain | 3.2 |
| Royal household | 5.0 |
| Administration | 2.5 |
| Other | 5.4 |

Total 249.8 million ducats

H. Kamen (**52**), p. 218, after Domínguez Ortiz (**21**).

# The Budget for 1690 **document 2**

| | Expenditure | Escudos Vellón | Percentage |
|---|---|---|---|
| *King's household* | | | |
| Household, chamber, wardrobe | 206,087 | | |
| Chapel | 44,000 | | |
| Lighting and medicine | 37,612 | | |
| Alms | 13,200 | | |
| Gentlemen and pages | 69,543 | | |
| Guards | 66,126 | | |
| Servants | 60,881 | | |
| Stables: provisions | 30,500 | | |
| personnel | 53,930 | | |
| | | 586,841 | 13 |
| *Queen's household* | | | |
| Ordinary expenses | 185,995 | | |
| Lighting | 15,882 | | |
| Chamber | 90,617 | | |
| Servants | 54,480 | | |
| Stables | 53,805 | | |
| | | 400,779 | 8.8 |
| Royal palaces | | 137,508 | 3.0 |
| Queen Mother's household | | 441,176 | 9.7 |
| Councils and Chanceries: salaries | | 412,334 | 9.1 |
| *Military and administrative* | | | |
| Invalid soldiers | 120,000 | | |
| Mail to Italy and Flanders | 38,880 | | |
| Garrisons in Spain | 188,265 | | |
| Other | 342,304 | | |
| | | 689,449 | 15.2 |
| *Financiers, for asientos** | | | |
| Don Francisco Eminente | 422,391 | | |
| Others | 526,042 | | |
| | | 948,433 | 20.9 |
| *Extraordinary payments* | | | |
| *Juristas**, pensions, widows | 149,585 | | |
| Officers: salaries, etc. | 61,707 | | |
| Alms, etc. | 39,934 | | |
| Other | 377,006 | | |
| | | 628,232 | 13.9 |
| *Special payments, all military* | | 286,814 | 6.4 |
| Total | | 4,531,566 | 100 |

H. Kamen (**48**), p. 368.

**document 3**

## Castile's unequal burden

*The Council of Finance complained that Castile bore the entire burden of the Monarchy (2 December 1618).*

The kingdoms of Aragon, Valencia and Catalonia contribute nothing to Your Majesty's expenses beyond their own frontiers, and money even has to be sent to them from Castile to pay their garrisons. Would Your Majesty please consider the possibility of discussing with the Council of Aragon whether these kingdoms could themselves undertake the provision of the money required for paying the troops garrisoned in them.... Everything is met out of the resources of Castile and out of what comes from the Indies, and literally nothing is contributed by Aragon, Valencia, Catalonia, Portugal and Navarre. As a result, Castile's revenues are pledged to the hilt, and it finds itself in such a state that one cannot see how it can possibly go on paying such vast sums.

Cited in J. H. Elliott (**24**), p. 190.

*This viewpoint was echoed in 1626 by the famous* arbitrista\*, *Fernández Návarrete:*

All monarchies have been accustomed to enrich the head of the empire with the spoils and tributes of provinces and nations won by arms or legitimately acquired by other means.... Only Castile has pursued a different method of government, because, while it should, as the head, be the most privileged in the payment of taxes, it is in fact the most heavily taxed of all, and contributes the largest sum to the Monarchy's defence.... It is only reasonable that the burdens should be distributed in proper proportion: that Castile should continue to provide for the royal household and for the defence of its own coasts and the route to the Indies; that Portugal should pay for its own garrisons and for the East Indies fleets, as it did before it was incorporated with Castile, and that Aragon and Italy should defend their coasts and maintain the necessary militia and ships for the purpose. It is quite unreasonable that the head should be weakened while the other members, which are very rich and populous, should simply stand by and look on while it has to bear all these heavy charges.

Cited in J. H. Elliott (**24**), p. 191.

**document 4**
## The Treasury budgets of Milan

*The figures, in* scudi, *indicate the extent of outside subsidies.*

| Year | (1)<br>Gross<br>receipts | (2)<br>Net<br>receipts | (3)<br>Expenses | (4)<br>Gross<br>shortfall | (5)<br>Outside<br>subsidies | (6)<br>Net<br>shortfall |
|------|------|------|------|------|------|------|
| 1641 | 1,321,264 | 0 | 2,948,026 | 2,948,026 | 827,266 | 2,120,760 |
| 1642 | 1,264,655 | 368,928 | 3,406,194 | 3,037,266 | 1,963,680 | 1,073,586 |
| 1643 | 1,250,242 | 373,881 | 3,059,107 | 2,685,226 | 1,130,957 | 1,554,269 |
| 1648 | 1,136,632 | 348,834 | 2,149,346 | 1,800,512 | 1,406,544 | 1,070,137 |
| 1657 | 1,191,175 | 269,184 | 2,394,619 | 2,125,435 | — | — |
| 1658 | 1,263,142 | 295,079 | 2,279,881 | 1,984,802 | — | — |

D. Sella (**87**), p. 65, reprinted by permission of the publisher.

**document 5**
## The Army of Flanders, 1607–61

| Date | Spaniards | Total infantry | Cavalry | Grand total |
|------|------|------|------|------|
| Mar. 1607 | 6,545 | 37,307 | 4,164 | 41,471 |
| Mar. 1609 | 6,528 | 13,759 | 1,500 | 15,259 |
| Aug. 1611 | 5,566 | 12,943 | 1,718 | 14,661 |
| May 1619 | 6,310 | 25,832 | 3,378 | 29,210 |
| Jun. 1620 | 10,449 | 37,196 | 7,004 | 44,200[1] |
| Mar. 1622 | 6,332 | | | 38,152 |
| Mar. 1623 | 3,739 | 55,207 | 7,399 | 62,606[1] |
| Apr. 1624 | 7,354 | 63,720 | 7,568 | 71,288[1] |
| Mar. 1626 | | | | 54,003 |
| Jan. 1627 | 6,077 | 62,525 | 6,815 | 69,340[2] |
| Feb. 1628 | | | | 34,762 |
| Sept. 1633 | 5,693 | 45,067 | 7,648 | 52,715 |
| Mar. 1636 | | | | 69,703 |

| Date | Spaniards | Total infantry | Cavalry | Grand total |
|------|-----------|----------------|---------|-------------|
| Jan.  1640 | 17,262 | 76,933 | 11,347 | 88,280 |
| Dec.  1643 | 10,438 | 63,422 | 14,095 | 77,517 |
| Feb.  1647 | 9,685 | 53,724 | 11,734 | 65,458 |
| Sept. 1661 | 5,481 | 25,024 | 7,984 | 33,008 |

[1] These figures include the Army of the Palatinate (which in 1620 amounted to 22,000 troops).

[2] This figure includes troops paid for locally, by the Spanish Netherlands' 'Finances' department. In 1623 these amounted to 15,722 men; therefore approximately this number should usually be added to the total in the other years.

*Source:* Compiled from G. Parker (**71**), p. 272, and J. Israel (**40**), p. 166, reproduced by permission of Oxford University Press.

**document 6**

## Spanish and Italian troops sent to the Netherlands, 1598–1640

| Years | Commander | Numbers and route | | |
|-------|-----------|-------------------|---|---|
| | | Spanish Road* | Alsace | Sea |
| 1598 | Leyva | — | — | 4,000 S |
| 1601 | Spinola | 2,000 S 6,000 I | — | — |
| 1601 | Girón | — | — | 1,500 S |
| 1602 | Spinola | 8,759 I | — | — |
| 1602 | F. Spinola | — | — | 1,000 S |
| 1603 | Borja | 2,500 S 1,200 I | — | — |
| 1604 | Biamonte | — | 2,000 S | — |
| 1605 | Girón | — | 2,877 S | — |
| 1605 | Avellino | 6,000 I | — | — |
| 1605 | Sarmiento | — | — | 1,200 S |
| 1606 | Bravo de Laguna | 3,000 S | — | — |
| 1611 | — | — | — | 500 S |
| 1615 | Vidalcanal | — | — | 2,924 S |
| 1620 | Oliveyra | — | — | 1,080 P |

| Years | Commander | Numbers and route | | |
|-------|-----------|---------|--------|------|
| | | Spanish Road* | Alsace | Sea |
| 1620 | Córdoba | 2,205 S | — | — |
| | | 6,395 I | | |
| 1623 | Claros de | — | 1,889 S | — |
| | Guzmán | | 4,969 I | |
| | | | 393 C | |
| 1623 | Medina | — | — | 1,500 S |
| 1631 | Santa Cruz | — | 9,782 SI | — |
| | | | 1,526 C | |
| 1631 | Jacobssen | — | — | 1,223 S |
| 1631 | Ribera | — | — | 4,367 S |
| 1634 | — | — | — | 1,200 S |
| 1634 | Cardinal infante | — | 9,540 SI | — |
| | | | 2,044 C | |
| 1635 | — | — | — | 2,000 S |
| 1636 | Velada | — | — | 3,671 S |
| 1637 | Hozes | — | — | 4,000 S |
| 1639 | B. Wright | — | — | 1,500 S |
| 1639 | Oquendo | — | — | 9,000 S |

C = cavalry; I = Italian infantry; P = Portuguese infantry; S = Spanish infantry

G. Parker (**71**), p. 278.

## Population in three Spanish cities

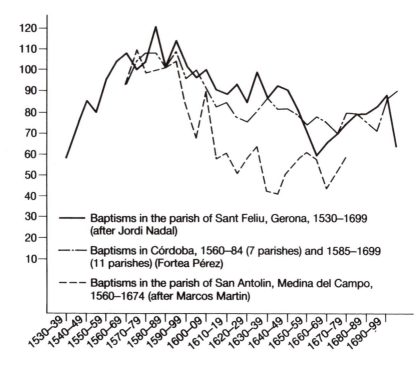

H. Kamen (**52**), p. 279 (base 100 = 1580–84).

## American treasure returns

| 1580–84 | 48.0 | 1620–24 | 50.0 | 1660–64 | 65.0 |
| 1585–89 | 43.2 | 1625–29 | 42.2 | 1665–69 | 61.3 |
| 1590–94 | 30.4 | 1630–34 | 39.8 | 1670–74 | 87.0 |
| 1595–99 | 78.4 | 1635–39 | 68.8 | 1675–79 | 84.5 |
| 1600–4 | 55.5 | 1640–44 | 45.2 | 1680–84 | 51.5 |
| 1605–9 | 51.8 | 1645–48 | 36.6 | 1685–89 | 78.0 |
| 1610–14 | 43.1 | 1650–54 | 39.0 | 1690–94 | 81.8 |
| 1615–19 | 47.4 | 1655–59 | 51.6 | 1695–99 | 65.5 |

In million pesos; J. Lynch (**63**), p. 283, from Morineau (**69**), p. 262.

**document 9**
## The Duke of Lerma

*In this letter the Cardinal of Toledo writes to Lerma, his great nephew (9 May 1600). The content refers to both the extent and criticisms of Lerma's power.*

The king applies himself freely to what [you] advise and ask for, and it is said that the [projected] removal to Vallodolid [will be on account of] the building of the church and palace there that Your Excellency desires and covets so vehemently.

[It is also said that] the king is taken to the countryside so that he shall not deal with anyone nor ascertain the multitude of virtues and good talents that there are in all kinds of his subjects. This same is said of the queen's household and of that of the king, that particular attention is taken of persons appointed by Your Excellency.... The current belief is that the people who can communicate and deal with Your Excellency are those who are favoured on account of the flatteries they afford Your Excellency, and everyone doubts their integrity and competence.... The observation must be made of Your Excellency that [you] indignantly and ungenerously ignore such warnings, counsels or petitions as are not to [your] taste, and that the replies and discussions on matters of business accord with the humour and pleasure in which Your Excellency finds himself, and not with their subject-matter.

Cited in P. Williams (**115**), pp. 763–4.

**document 10**
## The Truce between Spain and the Netherlands, 1609

*The observance of Clause Four concerning restrictions on commercial activity became an issue of dispute.*

The subjects and inhabitants of the countries of the said lord king, archdukes and estates shall have good relations and friendship with one another during the said Truce, without resenting the damage and harm that they have received in the past; they shall also be able to enter and to stay in one another's countries, and to exercise there their trade and commerce in full security both by sea and other waters as well as by land; however, the said king understands this to be restrained and limited to the kingdoms, countries, lands and lordships which he has and possesses in Europe and other places and seas in which the subjects of other princes who are his friends and allies have the said trade by mutual consent; as regards the places, towns, ports and harbours that he holds beyond the said limits, that the lords estates and their subjects may not carry on any trade without the express permission of the said lord king; but they shall be allowed to carry on the said trade, if it seems good to them, in countries of all other princes, potentates and peoples who may wish to permit them to do so even outside the said limits, without the said lord king, his officers and subjects who depend on him making any impediments in this event to the said princes, potentates and peoples who may have permitted it to them, nor equally to them [i.e the Dutch] or to the persons with whom they have carried out or will carry out the said trade.

J. Dumont, *Corps Universal Diplomatique de Droit de Gens*, vol. v, part 2, Amsterdam, 1728, pp. 99–102.

**document 11**

## Spain and the Truce

*Whether or not the Truce with the Dutch should be renewed or broken gener-ated considerable debate in the councils between 1618 and 1621. Both the Secretary to the Council of State, Juan de Ciriza, and the leading councillor, Baltasar de Zúñiga, felt the present terms should be improved.*

(I)
According to our information from Flanders, for several years the Dutch have been divided into parties: the maritime towns want war on account of their interest while the rest press for peace so as to be free of the taxes and burdens that war brings. Also it has been seen throughout that the truce was highly favourable to the Dutch and that since it was signed, they find themselves unhindered with overflowing wealth while these realms are much diminished, since the Dutch have taken their commerce, and that this damage, if not remedied, will daily become worse.

Ciriza, 2 March 1618

(II)
We cannot by force of arms, reduce those provinces to their former obedience. Whoever looks at the matter carefully and

without passion, must be impressed by the great armed strength of those provinces both by land and by sea, their strong geographical position ringed by the sea and by great rivers, lying close to France, England and Germany. Furthermore that state is at the very height of its greatness, while ours is in disarray. To promise ourselves that we can conquer the Dutch is to seek the impossible, to delude ourselves. To those who put all blame for our troubles on to the Truce and foresee great benefits from breaking it, we can say for certain that whether we end it or not we shall always be at a disadvantage. Affairs can get to a certain stage where every decision taken is for the worse, not through lack of good advice, but because the situation is so desperate that no remedy can conceivably be found. However it is also certain that, from the present Truce, which has not been properly applied as regards the Indies, have arisen those damaging consequences which we see. For this reason we must take more adequate measures in future.

Zúñiga, 7 April 1619

Both cited in P. Brightwell (9), pp. 277 and 289.

**document 12**

## An *Arbitrista**

*Martín González de Cellorigo, whose Memorial appeared in 1600, complained of the absence of people 'of the middling sort' and the lack of sound investment.*

Our republic has come to be an extreme contrast of rich and poor, and there is no means of adjusting them one to another. Our condition is one in which we have rich who loll at ease, or poor who beg, and we lack people of the middling sort, whom neither wealth nor poverty prevent from pursuing the rightful kind of business enjoined by natural law.

[At present, surplus wealth was being unproductively invested] – dissipated in thin air – on papers, contracts, *censos,** and letters of exchange, on cash, and silver, and gold – instead of being expended on things that yield profits and attract riches from outside to augment the riches within. And thus there is no money, gold, or silver in Spain because there is so much; and it is not rich, because of all its riches.

Cited in J. H. Elliott (23), pp. 310 and 317.

**document 13**
## Botero and unity

*In his famous work* Reason of State *(1589), Giovanni Botero discusses the pros and cons of a geographically dispersed state.*

Now we should say that without doubt a great empire is more safe from enemy attacks and invasions because it is powerful and united, and unity confers strength and firmness; yet on the other hand it is more vulnerable to the internal causes of ruin, for greatness leads to self-confidence, confidence to negligence and negligence to contempt and loss of prestige and authority.

On the other hand a scattered empire is weaker than a compact one because the distance between the parts is always a source of weakness and if the different parts are so weak that none of them is able to stand alone against the attacks of a neighbouring power, or if they are so placed that one cannot come to the aid of another, then the empire will not last long. But if they are able to help each other and if each is large and vigorous so that it need not fear invasion, the empire may be accounted as strong as a compact one.

From Giovanni Botero, *Reason of State*, trans. P. J. and D. P. Waley, Routledge and Kegan Paul, 1956, pp. 9, 11 (see also (**29**), p. 192).

**document 14**
## The Great Memorial

*Olivares exhorts the King to become 'King of Spain' (25 December 1624).*

The most important piece of business in your Monarchy is for Your Majesty to make yourself King of Spain. By this I mean, Sir, that Your Majesty should not be content with being King of Portugal, Aragon, and Valencia, and Count of Barcelona, but should work and secretly scheme to reduce these kingdoms of which Spain is composed to the style and laws of Castile, with no differentiation in the form of frontiers, customs posts, the power to convoke the Cortes of Castile, Aragon and Portugal wherever it seems desirable, and the unrestricted appointment of ministers of different nations both here and there. . . . And if Your Majesty achieves this, you will be the most powerful prince in the world.

*He suggests methods for securing closer union:*

The first, Sir, and the most difficult to achieve, but the best, if it can be achieved, would be for Your Majesty to favour natives of those kingdoms by introducing them into Castile, arranging marriages between them and Castilians, and so smoothing their way with favours that – with their admission into the offices and dignities of Castile – they forget their privileges in their enjoyment of those of Castile. In this way it would be possible to negotiate this most advantageous and necessary union.

From John H. Elliott and José F. de la Peña, *Memoriales y Cartas del Conde Duque de Olivares*, Ediciones Alfaguara, 1978, Vol. I pp. 96–7, cited in (**29**) pp. 196–80.

**document 15**
## The Union of Arms

*Olivares's quotas for his military reserve were as follows:*

| | |
|---|---:|
| Catalonia | 16,000 |
| Aragon | 10,000 |
| Valencia | 6,000 |
| Castile and the Indies | 44,000 |
| Portugal | 16,000 |
| Naples | 16,000 |
| Sicily | 6,000 |
| Milan | 8,000 |
| Flanders | 12,000 |
| Mediterranean and Atlantic islands | 6,000 |

From John H. Elliott and José F. de la Peña, *Memoriales y Cartas del Conde Duque de Olivares*, Ediciones Alfaguara, 1978, Vol. I p. 192, cited in (**29**) pp. 247–8.

Documents

## Philip IV triumphant

**document 16**

*Philip IV, in a message to the Council of Castile in 1626, is unable to disguise his jubilation at the events of 1625. His figures are slightly exaggerated.*

Our prestige has been immensely improved. We have had all Europe against us, but we have not been defeated, nor have our allies lost, whilst our enemies have sued me for peace. Last year, 1625, we had nearly 300,000 infantry and cavalry in our pay, and over 500,000 men of the militia under arms, whilst the fortresses of Spain are being put into a thorough state of defence. The fleet, which consisted of only seven vessels on my accession, rose at one time in 1625 to 108 ships of war at sea, without counting the vessels at Flanders, and the crews are the most skilful mariners this realm ever possessed. . . . This very year of 1626 we have had two royal armies in Flanders and one in the Palatinate, and yet all the power of France, England, Sweden, Venice, Savoy, Denmark, Holland, Brandenberg, Saxony, and Weimar could not save Breda from our victorious arms.

Cited in M. Hume (**37**), pp. 156–7.

## Peter Paul Rubens

**document 17**

*The famous Flemish painter spent eight months in Madrid in 1628–29, as an ambassador and an artist. This extract is part of a letter to Jan Caspar Gevaerts, a friend and scholar in Antwerp. He refers to the Dutch capture of the Spanish silver fleet and the King's personality.*

The loss of the fleet has caused great discussion here, but as long as no report comes from our side, we are unwilling to believe it. However, according to the general opinion it is only too true that the loss is enormous. It is imputed to folly and negligence rather than misfortune, since no precautions were taken, in spite of many timely warnings against the threatened disaster. You would be surprised to see that almost all the people here are very glad about it, feeling that this public calamity can be set down as a disgrace to their rulers. So great is the power of hate that they overlook or fail to feel their own ills, for the mere pleasure of vengeance.

The King alone arouses my sympathy. He is endowed by nature with all the gifts of body and spirit, for in my daily intercourse with him I have learned to know him thoroughly. And he would surely be capable of governing under any conditions, were it not that he mistrusts himself and defers too much to others. But now he has to pay for his own credulity and others' folly, and feel the hatred that is not meant for him. Thus have the gods willed it.

But I must break off, and bring an end to this letter and my fatigue, but not to my feeling for you. Farewell, excellent and incomparable man, and make daily prayers to Fortune for the return of your Rubens, whom you rightly love as a true friend. Once more, farewell.

Your humble and devoted servant,

Madrid, December 29, 1628                     Peter Paul Rubens

From R. S. Magurn (**64**), p. 295.

**document 18**

## Olivares blames Spinola

*In a voto of 1630 Olivares sought to blame all the setbacks of 1628–29 on Ambrosio Spinola, the Marquis of Los Bálbases.*

Your majesty has lost land and reputation in all parts because of the presumption and vehemence of the marquis's policies, which he insisted should be followed in Flanders and Italy, even to the extent of demanding to be captain-general in both places at once.... Everywhere he has been willing to sacrifice honour for peace, and we lost what we did in Flanders last year because of his assurances that the enemy were ready to negotiate.... It is of the greatest danger to your majesty's service that you should govern yourself in everything absolutely according to the marquis's opinions, against that of all the others. I beseech your majesty to recall what these setbacks of the last two years have cost us.

Cited in R. A. Stradling (**99**), p. 98.

## Medina de las Torres

*In this extract written in March 1639 the Duke complains that the Monarchy is overstretched.*

The concern caused me by the fall of Breisach and its consequences; the entry of French arms into Piedmont; the disturbances and dangers to which I see His Majesty's kingdoms exposed and the problems which the multiplication of taxes pose to his service ... inspire me to write these lines ... despite the danger to which I may expose myself, the ignorance or licence of which I may be accused by speaking in this way.... The kingdoms and states of our master are exhausted in the highest degree, and those that do not suffer war themselves bear the burden of taxes, the raising of levies, the imposition of billeting, the depopulation of the countryside, and the general extinction of prosperity. This responsibility is not divided equally, as it is with our enemies, with the result that only the crown of Castile, and the kingdoms of Naples and Sicily are required to offset all the revenues of France and the Estates of Holland and their adherents.... The conclusion must be that His Majesty cannot maintain this war much longer in its present form, nor expose all his kingdoms to such manifest peril, and must therefore by necessity seek out those means by which it may be possible to progress towards peace.

Cited in R. A. Stradling (**92**), p. 12.

*In these extracts written in (I) 1659 and (II) 1666, the Duke writes of human misery and true reputation.*

(I)
What is worst of all [he wrote in July 1659] is the condition of the countryside, the lack of cultivation of the fields. to such a degree that in Spain and Italy more than half the land is not farmed because of depopulation and deprivation. Unless we achieve peace we will find ourselves without people, without money, fleets, officers; without strongholds or munitions, in short without any means of defending ourselves.

(II)
The true reputation of states does not consist of mere appearances, but in the constant security and conservation of their territories, in the protection of their subjects and the wellbeing thereof, in the respect which other princes have for their authority and military strength.... Glorious actions are not founded in the vulgar vanity of words, but in deeds of substance.

Cited in R. A. Stradling (**92**), pp. 19–20.

**document 20**

**Olivares and Catalonia**

*In a letter dated 29 February 1640 to the Viceroy, Santa Coloma, Olivares expresses his indignation at the behaviour of the Catalans.*

I have never heard of anything so ridiculous as the behaviour of the *Diputació\** and the *Consell de Cent\** on this occasion. And forgive my language, which is the most restrained I can manage, but no king in the world has a province like Catalonia.... It has a king and lord, but it renders him no services, even when its own safety is at stake. This king and lord can do nothing that he wants in it, nor even things that need to be done. If the enemy invades it, the king has to defend it without any help from the inhabitants, who refuse to expose themselves to danger. He has to bring in an army from outside; he has to maintain it; he has to recover the fortresses that have been lost. And then, when the enemy has not yet been driven out... the province refuses to billet it.... We always have to look and see if a constitution says this or that. We have to discover what the customary usage is, even when it is a question of the supreme law, of the actual preservation and defence of the province.... Sir, we all admire your wisdom, but we all without exception consider that a viceroy of that province, and especially a native of it, like yourself, should have made an example of these people.... How is it possible that, of thirty-six ministers who have seen the despatches this morning, there is not one who is not clamouring, clamouring against Catalonia? ... Sir, the king our lord is king of Castile, which has billeted troops; he is king of Navarre, which has billeted and is today billeting them. He is king of Aragon, which is doing the same, and Valencia, too. He is king of Portugal, which, although one of those kingdoms with many *fueros*, has never objected to billeting. And Milan, Naples,

Flanders, the Indies, the Franche-Comté, than which there is probably no state or province with more liberties and immunities. Not one of these objects to billeting, not only when it is helping in its own defence but even when His Majesty chooses to station troops in it. Should all these kingdoms and provinces follow the example of Catalonia?...Really, Sir, the Catalans ought to see more of the world than Catalonia.

Cited in J. H. Elliott (**24**), pp. 400–1.

**document 21**

## Hopton and Besançon on 1640

*In a letter of April 1641 Sir Arthur Hopton, the British ambassador, vividly describes the spreading demoralization created by the two revolts of 1640.*

Concerning the state of this kingdom, I could never have imagined to have seen it as it now is, for their people begin to fail, and those that remain, by a continuance of bad success, and by their heavy burdens, are quite out of heart. They have not one man of quality fit to command an army. The king's revenues being paid in brass money will be lessened a third part being reduced to silver. They begin already to lay hands on the silver vessel of particular men, which, together with that in the churches, is all the stock of silver in the kingdom. Their trade must of necessity fail through the daily new burdens that are laid thereon, and the molestation of merchants.... Justice is quite extinguished here, and the people are become almost desperate, partly by the intolerable *sisas** they pay upon whatsoever they spend (bread only excepted) and partly by the great sums of money that are daily extorted from them. Their provisions of shipping and mariners are not the tenth part of what they have been and what they ought to be, and the greatest mischief of all is that the King of Spain knows little of all this, and the Count-Duke is so wilful as he will break rather than bend. So as your honour may be confident this monarchy is in great danger to be ruined, and whether that will be good for us and the rest of Christendom is best known to your honour.

Cited in J. H. Elliott (**29**), p. 611.

*Duplessis Besançon, Richelieu's agent in Catalonia, also describes the consequences.*

One can say without exaggeration that the consequences of this event were such that (apart from the revolt of Portugal, whose loss was so prejudicial not only to Spain's reputation but to the whole structure of its monarchy – and which would never have dared revolt without the Catalan example, since it was afraid of being rapidly overwhelmed if it engaged alone in so hazardous a dance) our affairs (which were not going well in Flanders, and still worse in Piedmont) suddenly began to prosper on all sides, even in Germany; for our enemy's forces, being retained in their own country and recalled from elsewhere to defend the sanctuary, were reduced to feebleness in all the other theatres of war.

Cited in J. H. Elliott (**24**), p. 523.

**document 22**

## Dutch losses to the Dunkirkers, 1642–44

| *Types of vessel captured or sunk* | *1642* | *1643* | *1644* |
|---|---|---|---|
| Warships | 1 (28 guns) | 1 (26 guns) | 1 (200 lasts; 32 guns) |
| Muscovy ships (*Moscouvaerders*) | 8 | – | – |
| *Straatvaarders* | 2 | – | 1 |
| East and West India ships | 2 | 1 | – |
| Fluits (over 150 lasts) | 11 | 18 | 10 |
| Fluits (100–150 lasts) | 26 | 15 | 10 |
| Fluits (under 100 lasts) | 12 | 4 | 1 |
| Smacks and boats (under 50 lasts) | 18 | 12 | 37 |
| Herring busses | 5 | 6 | 12 |
| Other fishing craft | 33 | 41 | 66 |
| Total | 118 | 98 | 138 |

From J. Israel (**40**), p. 327, reproduced by permission of Oxford University Press.

**document 23**
## Olivares confesses to the Venetian ambassador, 1641

*In a surprisingly frank confession to Niccolò Sagredo, the Venetian ambassador, Olivares revealed his inner thoughts.*

I must tell you in confidence that I have been the most ambitious man in the world. I confess that I never stopped machinating, I never slept at night, in the effort to advance my fortunes. I regarded the *privanza* as a state of incomparable felicity; I secured it; and I have held if for twenty years. And now – and God punish me if this is not the truth – my only desire is to conclude a peace, and then die. As regards the king, I owe him everything.... But for him I would almost not be a Christian, for whenever I pray to God it is for him.... As for myself, I would be content to conclude a peace and then die.... And here in my breast I have a sealed envelope whose contents describe the kind of life I have determined to live.

Cited in J. H. Elliott (**29**), p. 620–2.

**document 24**
## Luis de Haro, First Minister

*In a letter to his confidante, Sister María, Philip IV explains his decision to give Don Luis significant responsibility (1647).*

I have always told you of my intention to comply with God's wishes as regards my royal obligations, and I assure you once again here and now – a thousand and one times over.... But I am convinced that I should not infringe them in following the best example of my predecessors.... Philip the Second, my grandfather, the goodness of whose rule is acknowledged by all, took certain servants or ministers into his confidence, valuing them highly for their talents in advice and business, yet always reserving the last word for himself. This type of government has been used under many monarchies old and new, where there has never failed to be a principal minister or confident servant, with sufficient authority to ensure the carrying out of policy. Particularly at the present juncture, when speed and efficiency in the most serious matters are at a premium, I alone cannot perform what is necessary.... For example, it would be quite inappropriate for me to go from house to house amongst my ministers and secretaries, checking on their prompt and proper discharge of their duty, nor can I regularly interview all my servants to such ends. . . .

The person whom I have selected was brought up with me: I know him well, he has fine qualities, has worked hard, and is of good faith. As with others, I have refrained from giving him any special character, in order not to reproduce the basis of that earlier method of government whose evil I now firmly recognise. In particular I have entrusted him with fundraising tasks and expeditions to prepare campaigns, and to bring me news and honest reports – though others too have helped me in similar ways. . . . There are those who pretend to have more influence and authority than in reality I have given them; it is a natural delusion amongst men, but they should not be believed, since my resolution has not changed.

Cited in R. A. Stradling (**99**), p. 261.

*Sir Edward Hyde, in Madrid in 1650, compares the Duke of Medina de las Torres with Don Luis de Haro.*

He neither depended upon nor loved Don Lewis, being unlike him in his nature [and] had power enough with the king to do his own business, which was only to provide for his vast expenses, and being indeed the king's greatest confident in his walks of liberty. And so [he] never crossed Don Lewis in the general managery, and seldom came to the council except he was sent for; there being like-wise great suits between Don Lewis and him about some estate of the Duke of Olivares, which kept them from any intimate correspondence. . . . He was a man of parts, and wanted nothing to be a very good statesman but application, and he was industriously without that.

*And about Haro himself:*

He was as absolute a favourite . . . as any favourite of that age: nor was anything transacted at home or abroad but by his direction . . . yet . . . no man ever did so little alone. . . . In the most ordinary occurrences, which for the difficulty required little deliberation . . . he would give no order without formal consultation with the rest of the Council . . .

From the Earl of Clarendon, *History of the Rebellion*, ed. W. D. Macray, Clarendon Press, 1888, vol. V pp. 94, 92, cited in (**99**) pp. 263–4.

**document 25**

## Sister María de Ágreda

*Philip IV conducted a considerable correspondence with the Franciscan nun; this is a typical exchange (1645).*

All the parts of my Monarchy are in a terrible state, surrounded by wars and confusion in every quarter. But I believe that if only I could correct my own behaviour, everything will have its remedy.

From now on [responded Sor María] I and all my community will prostrate ourselves every day at the feet of the All-Highest, our faces to the floor, asking Him to look upon us [i.e., Spain] as a father; and be assured that His justice will be done.

God will not permit the Monarchy [returned Philip], which has done Him so many outstanding services in the perpetual defence of the Catholic religion, to seek its own downfall.

Cited in R. A. Stradling (**99**), p. 270.

**document 26**

## The battle of Rocroi, 1643

*The battle was a considerable defeat for Spain but it did not mark the end of Spanish power in the region. This account is taken from the* Mercure Français, *a semi-official digest.*

The armies were large; the shock of their encounter was great; the stubbornness with which both sides resisted was scarcely credible; the outcome was miraculous. Six thousand Spaniards were slain, five thousand seven hundred and thirty-seven were made prisoner. The booty taken by the French consisted of the baggage of the entire army; twenty cannon; a hundred and seventy-two banners, fourteen standards, and two pennants, which were presented to His Majesty by the sieur de Chevers. But the French lost two thousand men killed, including eighteen captains and lieutenants. There were many wounded, and few persons of distinction emerged without those honorable wounds that are the normal consequence of a hotly-disputed battle. The duke d'Enghien himself was hit five times by musket balls; two struck his cuirass, without having the force to penetrate it; two others hit his horse in the belly, obliging him to take another mount; the fifth grazed his leg, causing a contusion, but this did not prevent him from joining in the pursuit of the fleeing enemy. The officers of the highest rank who figured among the Spanish dead were: Count Fuentes, general of the armies of the king of Spain in the Netherlands; Don Antonio de Velandia; the counts of Villalva; Signor Visconti; and the baron d'Ambise, campmaster.

Cited in G. Symcox (**102**), pp. 140–1.

## Neapolitan subsidies to Milan

**document 27**

*The figures given are in Neapolitan ducats.*

| Anno | Monterrey | Anno | Medina |
|------|-----------|------|--------|
| 1631 | 305.000 | | |
| 1632 | 345.000 | 1638 | 1.148.000 |
| 1633 | 195.000 | 1639 | 1.350.000 |
| 1634 | 454.946 | 1640 | 800.000 |
| 1635 | 498.843 | 1641 | 1.350.000 |
| 1636 | 574.207 | 1642 | 1.219.969 |
| 1637 | 340.000 | 1643 | 630.000 |
| Totale | 2.712.997 | | 6.497.969 |

From G. Coniglio (**18**), *Il Viceregno di Napoli nel sec. XVII*, Edizionidi Storia e Le Letteratura, 1955, p. 272.

## The question of the succession

**document 28**

*Even prior to Philip IV's death, the French diplomat, Grémonville, was speculating about what might happen to the Spanish Monarchy if the sickly Charles were to die.*

1 The Spaniards might choose a native king, for example Don John of Austria, Philip IV's illegitimate son.
2 The papacy might try to seize the states of Naples and Sicily which were its fiefs, under the pretext of sequestering them.

111

3 The emperor might attempt to sequester Milan but could do so only with the consent of its Spanish and Swiss garrisons.
4 The Spanish Netherlands might be tempted to assert their independence.
5 There was some risk that the Indies might try to secede.

*He warned Louis XIV the following month (June 1665):*

There are members of the Emperor's Council so passionately devoted to the concept of an inseparable union of the two houses of Spain and Austria that they would take measures in Spain as well as trying to persuade His Imperial Majesty that his honour and dignity demand that he never give up Spain, if they perceived the slightest sign that Your Majesty intended to contest the succession or wanted to settle it by partition.

Cited in J. Bérenger (**3**), pp. 134 and 136.

**document 29**

## Don Juan of Austria

*This statement was found nailed to the door of the cathedral sacristy in Granada on 5 January 1669.*

Let all the residents of this city know that Don Juan of Austria, moved by holy concern, has written to all the cities of these realms about his just claims, moved at seeing the oppression of these poor subjects. In this city there is one who will rise to his defence, cutting off the heads of these tyrannical presidents and judges and sticking them on the battlements as a warning to others. The same will happen to the city council if they do not act justly and support his cause. These and other matters will be remedied from the start, and it will not be as in other times when we began and then left off at the best time. . . . With God's will all shall be remedied.

Cited in H. Kamen (**48**), p. 334.

# The inflation of honours

*The creation of Castilian nobles under Charles II.*

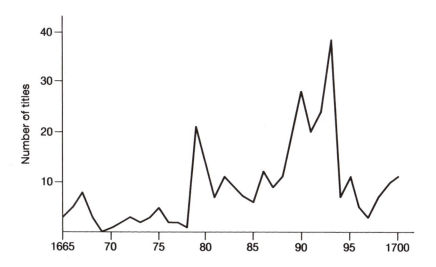

From H. Kamen **(48)**, p. 249.

# A calamitous year, 1683

*A report from the city authorities of Seville.*

The culmination of these afflictions came in the calamitous year of 1683, when drought left the fields barren and devoid of crops; food shortage became extremely critical, and people in their misery scratched the earth for grass and roots to keep alive.

*A report from the chronicler, Francisco Godoy.*

During the whole of 1683, until the end of November, there was not a drop of rain. Almost the whole of Andalucía was in absolute drought. The crops were parched with heat, the trees burnt up, cereals destroyed .... Bread became so scarce and expensive that many people perished of hunger. No one in Andalucía escaped privation. There was a stock farmer whose 1,600 head of cattle was

113

reduced to 200 because of drought and lack of fodder.... And I know another person who in addition to losing his cattle got only two bales of straw out of the 1,300 fanegas of grain he had sown.

Cited in J. Lynch (**63**), p. 394.

**document 32**

## The Castilian aristocracy

*The Venetian envoy, Fredrico Cornaro, reported in 1681:*

There is hardly a noble who does not live off the king's treasury or who, in the absence of royal pensions, could keep himself on his own income. Because of this, the principal lords, attracted by offices in Madrid, have abandoned their estates from which they draw empty titles rather than material benefit.

Cited in H. Kamen (**52**), p. 253.

*Again he stated in 1683:*

Bound together, one with another, by family ties and private interests for their mutual and separate advantage, they care nothing for the public weal nor for the good of the Crown. So much has their power increased and so much has that of the king diminished, that if he wanted to rule in a despotic and absolute manner ... it is difficult to see how he could succeed.

Cited in I. Thompson (**104**), p. 281.

*The French ambassador, Rébenac, reported in 1689:*

The king of Spain gives immense sums to the lords of his court. Pensions of thirty to fifty thousand pesos for idlers are common. It would seem natural to save this expense, but those who receive this money have nothing else to live on. They maintain a large number of servants in Madrid, and the consumption of Madrid is by itself the most substantial source of income for the king. Duties are about 300 to 400 per cent, so that what enters for one peso sells at four in the town. If the benefits of these people are cut back they will have to go to their estates, where it is impossible for them to live, since the countryside doesn't return one tenth of what it did forty years ago.

Cited in H. Kamen (**52**), p. 253.

**document 33**

## The will of Charles II, 1700

*Clauses 13 and 14:*

13. And recognizing, in accordance with the results of several consultations with our ministers of state and justice, that the reason for the renunciations by the Ladies *Donna Anna*[1] and *Donna Maria Teresa*,[2] Queens of France (my aunt and my sister), to the succession of these kingdoms, was to avoid the danger that these kingdoms would be joined to the Crown of France; but recognizing as well that if this basic reason should no longer operate, the right of succession remains to the closest relative, in accordance with the laws of our kingdoms, and that today this law is fulfilled in the case of the second son of the Dauphin of France; for this reason, and in accordance with the said laws, we declare as our successor (in the event that God should call us to Him without leaving issue) the *Duke of Anjou*, second son of the Dauphin; and in this quality, we call him to the succession to our realms and lordships, without excepting any part of them; and we declare and order all our subjects and vassals in all our realms and lordships, that in the above-mentioned case, if God gather us to Himself without legitimate heir, they receive and recognize him as their King and natural lord, and that he be given immediate possession, without any delay, once he has sworn to uphold the laws, immunities, and customs of our said realms and lordships; and since it is our intention, and it is also requisite for the peace of Christendom, and all Europe, and for the tranquillity of our kingdoms, that this Monarchy remain for ever separate from the Crown of France, we declare as a consequence of what has been said, that in the event that the Duke of Anjou should die, or inherit the Crown of France, and that he should prefer the enjoyment of that monarchical right to this, then in such a case the succession should pass to the *Duke of Berry* his brother, third son of the Dauphin, in the same manner and form; and in the event that the Duke of Berry should die, or

[1] Daughter of Philip III and wife of Louis XIII.
[2] Wife of Louis XIV and mother of the Dauphin: died 1683.

succeed to the Crown of France, then in that case we declare, and call to the succession, the *Archduke*, second son to our uncle, the Emperor; excluding, by reason of the same disabilities, as being contrary to the welfare of our subjects and vassals, the first son born to our uncle, the Emperor; and if the Archduke should fail to succeed, in this case we declare and call to the succession the *Duke of Savoy and his children*, it being our will that all our subjects and vassals carry this out and obey it, as we have ordered, as being requisite for their tranquillity, without there being the least dismemberment or diminution of the Monarchy so gloriously founded by our predecessors. And since we ardently desire that the peace and unity so needful to Christendom be maintained between our uncle, the Emperor, and the Most Christian King, we ask and exhort them to cement this said union by the marriage of the Duke of Anjou and the Archduchess, that by this means Europe may enjoy the peace that it so urgently needs.

14. And in the event that we should have no heir, the said Duke of Anjou is to succeed to all our kingdoms and lordships, not merely those belonging to the Crown of Castile, but also those of the Crowns of Aragon and Navarre, and to all our possessions both within and without Spain; notably, as concerns the Crown of Castile, Leon, Toledo, Galicia, Seville, Granada, Cordova, Murcia, Jaen, the Algarve, Alguire, Gibraltar, the Canary Isles, the Indies, the Islands and Mainland of the Ocean Sea of the North and South, the Philippines and other Islands, both lands already discovered and those to be discovered in the future, and all the rest of the possessions held by the Crown of Castile. And as concerns the Crown of Aragon, in our realms and states of Aragon, Valencia, Catalonia, Naples, Sicily, Majorca, Minorca, Sardinia, and all other lordships and rights belonging in any manner to that royal Crown. And in our state of Milan and our Duchies of Brabant, Limbourg, Luxembourg, Gelderland, Flanders, and all other states, provinces, dominions and lordships that belong to us or could belong to us in the Netherlands, rights and other possessions that have devolved upon us by reason of the succession to those said states. We wish that as soon as God has called us from this life, the Duke of Anjou be called to be King, as he shall be *ipso facto* by all, notwithstanding any renunciations and acts to the contrary, since they are without proper cause and foundation.

Cited in G. Symcox (**102**), pp. 65–7.

# Glossary

*Arbitristas*  Writers who suggested *arbitrios* or proposals for economic and political reform.

*Asiento*  A contract, often used to refer to the *asiento de dinero*, the money loans negotiated annually with the royal bankers (who were called *asientistas*). It can also refer to the rights to the slave trade.

*Audiencia*  Royal judicial tribunal – a high court of appeal.

*Bankruptcy*  The term is usually used to refer to a suspension of payments and the conversion of short-term loans into long-term ones.

*Bullion shipments*  There were two silver fleets each year – one from Tierra Firme (South America) known as the *galeones*, and one from New Spain (Mexico) known as the *flota*.

*Censo(s)*  Annuities drawn from loans.

*Cleves-Jülich*  Two duchies within the Holy Roman Empire subject to a disputed succession. The crisis (1609–14) ended in compromise; a Catholic, Wolfgang William of Neuberg, secured Jülich and Berg, and a Protestant, John Sigismund of Brandenburg, received Cleves and Mark.

*Consell de Cent*  The Council of One Hundred; the city council of Barcelona.

*Conservación*  A policy aimed at preserving and defending all the territories of the Spanish crown.

*Consulta*  A conciliar report summarizing deliberations sent to the King for information or action.

*Conversos*  Jews and Moors who were converted to Christianity.

*Cortes*  The parliament of each realm in the Iberian peninsula.

*Defenestration of Prague*  On 23 May 1618 two Catholic regents and their secretary were thrown out of the window of the royal palace (they landed in a dung heap and survived!). This gesture of defiance by the Bohemian nobles is usually considered to be the beginning of the Thirty Years War.

*Diputació*  A standing commission of six persons representing the Catalan parliament.

*Donativo*   A donation to the treasury, but not spontaneous; also a subsidy voted by the parliaments of Naples and Sicily.

*Ducat (ducado)*   See note on coinage, page v.

*Emperor*   The title Holy Roman Emperor conferred little actual power, but a nominal authority over Germany, which was itself divided into a myriad of states. From the middle of the fifteenth century it had been customary to elect a Habsburg as Emperor.

*Escudo*   See note on coinage, page v.

*Fuero(s)*   (A) legal privilege(s) – usually used in reference to the non-Castilian kingdoms of Spain.

*Grandeza*   Collective term for the grandees, the highest level of nobility.

*Hidalgo*   The lowest level of nobility.

*Jornada*   Royal journey or 'progress'.

*Junta*   A small committee of advisers.

*Juro*   Annuity paid out of state income for loans to the crown.

*Letrado*   Graduate in law who usually served in the royal bureaucracy.

*Media anata*   Tax on government salary and dividends; in effect, a reduced payment.

*Mercedes*   Rewards from the crown.

*Millones*   A tax on basic items – meat, wine, oil and vinegar – voted by the Cortes.

*Monarquía española*   The dominions of the Spanish crown, not called an empire, a title strictly reserved for the Holy Roman Empire.

*Morisco*   A Christianized Moor.

*Presidio(s)*   Fortified outposts in Africa and (mainly) Italy (adjacent to Tuscany).

*Reputación*   The Monarchy's prestige, image, standing and so forth.

*Servicio*   A grant of taxes by the Cortes.

*Sisa*   Tax on food.

*Spanish Road*   The route from Italy to Flanders for soldiers and supplies to that area (see Map 2, page 48).

*Tercio*   Infantry regiment in the Spanish army of about 1,000 men.

*Valido*   Royal favourite and Chief Minister, sometimes referred to as a *privado*.

*Valtelline*   An Alpine valley area important for communications between Milan and Vienna, and Milan and Brussels.

*Vellón*   See note on coinage, page v.

*Whig history*   Seeing the past from the present point of view; that is, distortion of the past by hindsight. So called after the essay by Sir Herbert Butterfield, *The Whig Interpretation of History* (1931).

# Bibliography

1   Alcalá-Zamora y Queipo de Llano, José, *España, Flandes y el mar del norte, 1618–1639,* Barcelona, 1975.
2   Astarita, Tommaso, *The Continuity of Feudal Power. The Caracciolo di Brienza in Spanish Naples,* Cambridge University Press, 1992.
3   Bérenger, Jean, 'An Attempted *Rapprochement* between France and the Emperor: the Secret Treaty for the Partition of the Spanish Succession of 19 January 1668', in Hatton, R. (ed.), *Louis XIV and Europe,* Macmillan, 1976, pp. 133–52.
4   Bonney, Richard, *The King's Debts. Finance and Politics in France 1589–1661,* Oxford University Press, 1981.
5   Bonney, Richard, *The European Dynastic States 1494–1660,* Oxford University Press, 1991.
6   Bonney, Richard, 'The Sinews of Power: the Finances of the French Monarchy from Henry IV to Louis XIV', *History Review,* 12 (1992), pp. 7–12.
7   Boyajian, James C., *Portuguese Bankers at the Madrid Court, 1626–1650,* Rutgers University Press, 1982.
8   Braudel, F., *The Mediterranean and the Mediterranean World in the Age of Philip II* (2 vols), William Collins, 1972.
9   Brightwell, P., 'The Spanish System and the Twelve Years Truce', *English Historical Review,* 89 (1974), pp. 270–92.
10  Brightwell, P., 'The Spanish Origins of the Thirty Years War', *European Studies Review,* 9 (1979), pp. 409–31.
11  Brightwell, P., 'Spain and Bohemia: the Decision to Intervene', *European Studies Review,* 12 (1982), pp 117–41.
12  Brightwell, P., 'Spain, Bohemia and Europe, 1619–21', *European Studies Review,* 12 (1982), pp. 371–99.
13  Calabria, Antonio, *Good Government in Spanish Naples,* ed. with John A. Marino, Peter Lang, 1990.
14  Calabria, Antonio, *The Cost of Empire: the Finances of the Kingdom of Naples during the Period of Spanish Rule,* Cambridge University Press, 1991.

15 Casey, James, *The Kingdom of Valencia in the Seventeenth Century*, Cambridge University Press, 1979.

16 Chaunu, Pierre and Huguette, 'The Atlantic Economy and the World Economy', in Earle, P. (ed.), *Essays in European History*, Oxford University Press, 1974, pp. 113–26.

17 Clark, George, 'The Nine Years War, 1688–97, in *The New Cambridge Modern History*, vol. VI, Cambridge University Press, 1970, pp. 223–53.

18 Coniglio, Giuseppe, *Il Viceregno di Napoli nel sec. XVII*, Edizioni di Storia e Letteratura, 1955.

19 Cooper, J.P. (ed.) *The New Cambridge Modern History*, vol. IV, Cambridge University Press, 1970.

20 Corbett, Julian S., *England and the Mediterranean* (2 vols), Longman, 1904.

21 Domínguez Ortiz, Antonio, *Política y Hacienda de Felipe IV*, Editorial de Derecho Financiero, 1960.

22 Domínguez Ortiz, Antonio, *The Golden Age of Spain 1516–1659*, Weidenfeld & Nicolson, 1971.

23 Elliott, John H., *Imperial Spain, 1469–1716*, Edward Arnold, 1963.

24 Elliott, John H., *The Revolt of the Catalans: a Study in the Decline of Spain, 1598–1640*, Cambridge University Press, 1963.

25 Elliott, John H., *A Palace for a King: the Buen Retiro and the Court of Philip IV* (with Jonathan Brown), Yale University Press, 1980.

26 Elliott, John H., Review of Henry Kamen's *Spain in the Later Seventeenth Century*, *Journal of Modern History*, 54 (1982), pp. 149–51.

27 Elliott, John H., 'A Question of Reputation? Spanish Foreign Policy in the Seventeenth Century', *Journal of Modern History*, 55 (1983), pp. 475–83.

28 Elliott, John H., *Richelieu and Olivares*, Cambridge University Press, 1984.

29 Elliott, John H., *The Count-Duke of Olivares: the Statesman in an Age of Decline*, Yale University Press, 1986.

30 Elliott, John H., *Spain and its World, 1500–1700*, Yale University Press, 1989.

31 Elliott, John H., 'The Spanish Monarchy and the Kingdom of Portugal, 1580–1640', in Greengrass, M. (ed.), *Conquest and Coalescence: the Shaping of the State in Early Modern Europe*, Edward Arnold, 1991, pp. 48–67.

**32**  Garzón Pareja, Manuel, *La Hacienda de Carlos II*, Instituto de Estudios Fiscales, 1980.

**33**  Hamilton, Earl J., *American Treasure and the Price Revolution in Spain, 1501–1650*, Harvard University Press, 1934.

**34**  Hamilton, Earl J., 'The Decline of Spain', *Economic History Review*, 8 (1938), pp. 168–79.

**35**  Hamilton, Earl J., *War and Prices in Spain 1651–1800*, Harvard University Press, 1947.

**36**  Howat, G. M. D., *Stuart and Cromwellian Foreign Policy*, Adam & Charles Black, 1974.

**37**  Hume, Martin, *The Court of Philip IV: Spain in Decadence*, Eveleign, Nash & Grayson, 1907.

**38**  Hussey, Roland Dennis, 'The Spanish Empire under Foreign Pressures, 1688–1715' in *The New Cambridge Modern History*, vol. VI, Cambridge University Press, 1970, pp. 343–80.

**39**  Israel, Jonathan I., 'The Decline of Spain: a Historical Myth?', *Past and Present*, 91 (1981), pp. 170–80.

**40**  Israel, Jonathan I., *The Dutch Republic and the Hispanic World 1606–1661*, Oxford University Press, 1982.

**41**  Israel, Jonathan I., Review of R. A. Stradling's *Philip IV*, *English Historical Review*, 104 (1989), p. 986.

**42**  Israel, Jonathan I., *Empires and Entrepots: the Dutch, the Spanish Monarchy and the Jews, 1585–1713*, The Hambledon Press, 1990.

**43**  Jago, Charles J., 'Habsburg Absolutism and the Cortes of Castile', *American Historical Review*, 86 (1981), pp. 307–26.

**44**  Jones, J. R., *Britain and Europe in the Seventeenth Century*, Edward Arnold, 1966.

**45**  Kagan, Richard L., *Lawsuits and Litigants in Castile, 1500–1700*, University of North Carolina Press, 1981.

**46**  Kamen, Henry, *The War of Succession in Spain 1700–15*, Weidenfeld & Nicolson, 1969.

**47**  Kamen, Henry, 'The Decline of Spain – a Historical Myth?', *Past and Present*, 81 (1978), pp. 24–81.

**48**  Kamen, Henry, *Spain in the Later Seventeenth Century 1665–1700*, Longman, 1980.

**49**  Kamen, Henry, 'The Decline of Spain – a Historical Myth? A Rejoinder', *Past and Present*, 91 (1981), pp. 181–85.

**50**  Kamen, Henry, *Golden Age Spain*, Macmillan, 1988.

**51**  Kamen, Henry, 'Early Modern Spain: the Difficulties of Empire', *History Sixth*, 2 (1988), pp. 2–6.

52  Kamen, Henry, *Spain 1469–1714: a Society of Conflict*, Longman, 2nd edn, 1991.
53  Kiernan, V. G., *State and Society in Europe 1550–1650*, Blackwell, 1980.
54  Knecht, R. J., *Richelieu*, Profiles in Power, Longman, 1991.
55  Koenigsberger, H. G., 'The Revolt of Palermo in 1647', *Cambridge Historical Journal*, 8 (1946), pp. 129–44.
56  Koenigsberger, H. G., *The Practice of Empire*, Cornell University Press, 1969. Emended version of *The Government of Sicily under Philip II of Spain* (1951).
57  Koenigsberger, H. G., *The Habsburgs and Europe 1516–1660*, Cornell University Press, 1971, containing 'The Empire of Charles V in Europe' and 'Western Europe and the Power of Spain' from vols I and II of *The New Cambridge Modern History*.
58  Lario Ramirez, Damaso de, *El Comte – Duc D'Olivares i el Regne de Valéncia*, Eliseu Climent, 1986.
59  Lockyer, Roger, *Buckingham: the Life and Political Career of George Villiers, First Duke of Buckingham, 1592–1628*, Longman, 1981.
60  Lovett, A. W., *Early Habsburg Spain 1517–1598*, Oxford University Press, 1986.
61  Lynch, John, *Spain under the Habsburgs*, vol. 2: *Spain and America 1598–1700*, Basil Blackwell, 2nd edn, 1981.
62  Lynch, John, *Bourbon Spain 1700–1808*, Basil Blackwell, 1989.
63  Lynch, John, *The Hispanic World in Crisis and Change 1598–1700*, Basil Blackwell, 1992. (This is, in effect, a third edition of **61**.)
64  Magurn, Ruth Saunders (trans. and ed.), *The Letters of Peter Paul Rubens*, Harvard University Press, 1955.
65  Mantelli, Roberto, *Il pubblico impiego nell' economia del Regno di Napoli: Retribuzioni, reclutamento e ricambio sociale nell' epoca spagnuola (secc. XVI–XVII)*, Nella Sede Dell' Istituto, 1986.
66  Marino, John A., *Pastoral Economics in the Kingdom of Naples*, Johns Hopkins University Press, 1988 (see also Calabria, Antonio).
67  McCusker, John J., *Money and Exchange in Europe and America, 1600–1775: a Handbook*, University of North Carolina Press, 1978.
68  McKay, Derek, *The Rise of the Great Powers 1648–1815* (with H. M. Scott), Longman, 1983.

**69** Morineau, Michel, *Incroyables gazettes et fabuleux métaux. Les retours des trésors américains d'après les gazettes hollandaises (XVI–XVIII siècles)*, Cambridge University Press, 1985.

**70** Nader, Helen, *Liberty in Absolutist Spain: the Habsburg Sale of Towns 1516–1700*, Baltimore, 1990.

**71** Parker, N. Geoffrey, *The Army of Flanders and the Spanish Road*, Cambridge University Press, 1972.

**72** Parker, N. Geoffrey, *An Introduction to the Sources of European Economic History 1500–1800* (ed. with Wilson, C.), Methuen, 1977.

**73** Parker, N. Geoffrey, *Philip II*, Little Brown, 1978.

**74** Parker, N. Geoffrey, *Europe in Crisis 1598–1648*, Harvester Press, 1979.

**75** Parker, N. Geoffrey, (*et al.*) *The Thirty Years War*, Routledge & Kegan Paul, 1984.

**76** Parker, N. Geoffrey, 'The Decline of Spain', *History Today*, April 1984, pp. 42–4.

**77** Parker, N. Geoffrey, *The Military Revolution: Military Innovation and the Rise of the West, 1500–1800*, Cambridge University Press, 1988.

**78** Parker, N. Geoffrey, *Spain and the Netherlands 1559–1659*, Fontana; revised edn, 1990.

**79** Parrott, David, 'The Causes of the Franco-Spanish War of 1635–59', in *The Origins of War in Early Modern Europe*, ed. Black, J., John Donald, 1987, pp. 72–111.

**80** Phillips, Carla Rahn, *Ciudad Real, 1500–1750*, Harvard University Press, 1979.

**81** Phillips, Carla Rahn, *Six Galleons for the King of Spain: Imperial Defense in the Early Seventeenth Century*, Johns Hopkins University Press, 1986.

**82** Phillips, Carla Rahn, 'Time and Duration: a Model for the Economy of Early Modern Spain', *American Historical Review*, 92 (1987), pp. 531–62.

**83** Pincus, Steven C. A., 'Popery, Trade and Universal Monarchy', *English Historical Review*, 107 (1992), pp. 1–29.

**84** Ranke, Leopold von, *The Ottoman and Spanish Empires in the Sixteenth and Seventeenth Centuries*, London, 1843.

**85** Reglá, Juan, 'Spain and her Empire', in *The New Cambridge Modern History*, vol. V, Cambridge University Press, 1961, pp. 369–83.

**86** Roosen, William, 'The Origins of the War of the Spanish Succession', in *The Origins of War in Early Modern Europe*, ed. Black, J., John Donald, 1987, pp. 151–75.

87  Sella, Domenico, *Crisis and Continuity: the Economy of Spanish Lombardy in the Seventeenth Century*, Harvard University Press, 1979.

88  Serrão, J. V., *Historia de Portugal*, vols IV and V, Lisbon, 1979–80.

89  Shennan, J. H., *Louis XIV*, Methuen, 1986.

90  Sonnino, Paul, *Louis XIV and the Origins of the Dutch War*, Cambridge University Press, 1988.

91  Stoye, John, *Europe Unfolding 1648–1688*, William Collins, 1969.

92  Stradling, R. A., 'A Spanish Statesman of Appeasement: Medina de las Torres and Spanish Policy, 1639–1670', *Historical Journal*, 19 (1976), pp. 1–31.

93  Stradling, R. A., 'Seventeenth-century Spain: Decline or Survival?', *European Studies Review*, 9 (1979), pp. 157–94.

94  Stradling, R. A., 'Catastrophe and Recovery: the Defeat of Spain, 1639–43', *History*, 64 (1979), pp. 205–19.

95  Stradling, R. A., *Europe and the Decline of Spain: a Study of the Spanish System, 1580–1720*, Allen & Unwin, 1981.

96  Stradling, R. A., 'Philip IV and the Survival of Spain', *History Today*, March 1981, pp. 16–23.

97  Stradling, R. A., 'Domination and Dependence: Castile, Spain, and the Spanish Monarchy', *European History Quarterly*, 14 (1984), pp. 77–91.

98  Stradling, R. A., 'Olivares and the Origins of the Franco-Spanish War, 1627–35', *English Historical Review*, 101 (1986), pp. 68–94.

99  Stradling, R. A., *Philip IV and the Government of Spain, 1621–1665*, Cambridge University Press, 1988.

100  Stradling, R. A., 'Kings of Lead in an Age of Gold? The Reputation of the Later Spanish Habsburgs', *History Sixth*, 5 (1989), pp. 6–11.

101  Stradling, R. A., 'Prelude to Disaster: the Precipitation of the War of Mantuan Succession, 1627–29', *Historical Journal*, 33 (1990), pp. 769–85.

102  Symcox, Geoffrey (ed.), *War, Diplomacy and Imperialism 1618–1763*, Harper & Row, 1973.

103  Taylor, Harland, 'Trade, Neutrality and the "English Road", 1630–1648', *Economic History Review*, 25 (1972), pp. 236–60.

104  Thompson, I. A. A., *War and Government in Habsburg Spain, 1560–1620*, Athlone Press, 1976.

105  Thompson, I. A. A., Review of Henry Kamen's *Spain in the Later Seventeenth Century*, *History*, 66 (1981), p. 521.

**106** Thompson, I. A. A., 'Crown and Cortes in Castile, 1590–1665', *Parliaments, Estates and Representation*, 2 (1982), pp. 29–45.

**107** Thompson, I. A. A., 'The End of the Cortes of Castile', *Parliaments, Estates and Representation*, 4 (1984), pp. 125–33.

**108** Thompson, I. A. A., Review of J. H. Elliott's *Olivares, English Historical Review*, 103 (1988), pp. 678–80.

**109** Thompson, I. A. A., Review of R. A. Stradling's *Philip IV, The Times Literary Supplement* (3 January 1989), p. 44.

**110** Thompson, I. A. A., 'Castile', in Miller, J. (ed.), *Absolutism in Seventeenth Century Europe*, Macmillan, 1990, pp. 69–98.

**111** Trevor-Roper, H. R., 'Spain and Europe 1598–1621', *The New Cambridge Modern History*, vol. IV, Cambridge University Press, 1970, pp. 260–82.

**112** Viçens Vives, J., 'The Administrative Structure of the State in the Sixteenth and Seventeenth Centuries', in Cohn, H. J. (ed.), *Government in Reformation Europe 1520–1560* (1971), pp. 58–87.

**113** Vilar, Jean, *Literatura y economía*, Madrid, 1973.

**114** Villari, Rosario, *La Revuelta Antiespañola de Nápoles: Los Origines (1585–1647)*, Alianza Editorial, 1979.

**115** Williams, P., 'Philip III and the Restoration of Spanish Government, 1598–1603', *English Historical Review*, 88 (1973), pp. 751–69.

**116** Williams, P., 'Lerma, Old Castile and the Travels of Philip III of Spain', *History*, 73 (1988), pp. 379–97.

**117** Williams, P., 'Lerma, 1618: Dismissal or Retirement?', *European History Quarterly*, 19 (1989), pp. 307–32.

**118** Wolf, John B., *Louis XIV*, Victor Gollancz, 1968.

# Index

# Index